Your Towns and Cities in the

Keswick
in the Great War

Your Towns and Cities in the Great War

Keswick
in the Great War

Ruth Mansergh

For my dad, the late John Tyson Mansergh (school teacher), and my granddad, Peter William Weightman (1920-2005). Also in memory of Dame Ann Brewer (nee Tyson) of Melbourne, who passed away peacefully in 2013

First published in Great Britain in 2016 by
PEN & SWORD MILITARY
an imprint of
Pen and Sword Books Ltd
47 Church Street
Barnsley
South Yorkshire S70 2AS

ISBN 978 1 47384 862 7

A CIP record for this book is available from the British Library.

Printed and bound in England
by CPI Group (UK) Ltd, Croydon, CR0 4YY

Typeset in Times New Roman

Pen & Sword Books Ltd incorporates the imprints of
Pen & Sword Archaeology, Atlas, Aviation, Battleground, Discovery,
Family History, History, Maritime, Military, Naval, Politics, Railways,
Select, Social History, Transport, True Crime, and Claymore Press,
Frontline Books, Leo Cooper, Praetorian Press, Remember When,
Seaforth Publishing and Wharncliffe.
For a complete list of Pen and Sword titles please contact
Pen and Sword Books Limited
47 Church Street, Barnsley, South Yorkshire, S70 2AS, England
E-mail: enquiries@pen-and-sword.co.uk
Website: **www.pen-and-sword.co.uk**

Contents

Author biography

Ruth Mansergh is a full-time mother of two who has worked as a journalist and as a freelance sub-editor/proofreader. She was brought up in Cumbria, went to school in North Yorkshire, and has a degree in English with Social History from Leeds University.

Acknowledgements

Thanks to my partner Alan McClenaghan for his computer wizardry with Photoshop. I am also grateful to local historians for their generosity and willingness to proofread copy. Very special thanks goes to Ian Stuart Nicholson for his invaluable help and to my university lecturer Cyril Pearce for sharing information. I have made every effort to contact copyright holders where appropriate and will be happy to update any omissions in any future edition of this book.

Introduction

The Keswick War Memorial on the corner of Penrith Road and Station Street, unveiled in 1922, commemorates 109 names from a population at the time of 4,043 (1911 census). On the memorial is a panel for seven men employed by the Cockermouth, Keswick & Penrith Railway Company (CK & PR) who lost their lives in the First World War.

In Keswick in September 1914, there were defence strategies for Thirlmere reservoir (Manchester water supply) and the third of four Thirlmere-Manchester pipe-lines was completed in 1915. Manchester had an insatiable appetite for water so it was seen as essential to wartime production to carry on.Force Crag Mine – part of the Keswick Mining Field – was worked with some vigour in the war. Its barytes deposits were in great demand by the newly-created Ministry of Munitions (1915).

On 5 November 1914, there were forty Belgian refugees at Keswick. Lord Rochdale owned the large house, Lingholm, on the western shore of Derwentwater, which was a Voluntary Aid Detachment (VAD) hospital in the war, providing nursing services. The VAD was the largest of the wartime organisations which provided nurses and orderlies at

The Keswick Convention, 1914.

home and on the fighting fronts. A number of Keswick women worked at HM Factory, Gretna, the UK's largest cordite factory during the Great War. On the other hand, conferences still drew people to the town, weddings continued, and 'boon' clips, when neighhours and friends gathered at a farm to shear the sheep, continued.

The First World War produced some of the most gifted and progressive authors, poets, social thinkers and artists of a generation and many lived in Keswick. The Reverend Hardwicke Rawnsley, who was moved to St Kentigern's Church, Crosthwaite in 1883 and formed the Keswick School of Industrial Art (KSIA) in 1884, had a passion for poetry. On 27 July, 1915, he had filled a volume with his verse for the times, which he called *The European War 1914-15* (Century Press). The sculptor Francis Derwent Wood was born in Keswick in 1871, volunteered in hospital wards at the onset of World War One and after the war became Professor of Sculpture at the Royal Academy of Arts, London. The No-Conscription Fellowship received support from suffrage campaigner Catherine Marshall of Keswick. Novelist Sir Hugh Walpole, who moved into a house near Keswick in 1923, was an ambulance driver in World War One. He served in the Red Cross on the Austro-Russian front.

The Moot Hall dominates Keswick's main street, and there are reports of a significant building on the site as early as 1571. This was at a time when German miners working copper and the activities of the Company of Mines Royal were boosting the prosperity of the 'lytle poore market town' (as described by English poet John Leland, 1530s) previously depending on wool for its livelihood. Within the first year of their residence, fourteen of the Germans married local girls. The names of Hindmarch, Stanger, and Pepper are still common in the area.

The hall – described by writer Norman Nicholson (1914-1987), a writer from Millom (Cumbria), in 1972 as 'a building so slim that you would expect a run-away bus to split on it like a ship on a rock' – was rebuilt in 1813. The Greta, a relative trickle, runs through Keswick to the River Derwent.

German miners sorting copper ore, sixteenth century.

Moot Hall now carefully adapted as a National Park Information Centre. *(Lake District National Park)*

Nicholson in Portrait of the Lakes (1972) wrote the following about Keswick:

'No other town in the district – none, in fact, England – is so fitted to become a tourist metropolis. The dale, the two lakes, the fells are

River Greta in Fitz Park, Keswick, with Penrith Road on the right.

Derwentwater, south of Keswick, is three miles long by one-and-a-quarter miles wide, and is the third largest of the Cumbrian lakes.
(Lake District National Park)

> laid out in front of you, giving up their great views without asking the payment of five minutes' effort. Skiddaw, the most obligingly demonstrative mountain in Cumberland, is so accessible that the Victorian ladies ascended it on pony-back.'

However, he said there had been attempts, here and there, to jazz-up the town as if it were the promenade at Morecambe.

Chapter 1

Recruits needed

On Sunday 2 August 1914, an appeal against panic was voiced by the Reverend Hardwicke Rawnsley of St Kentigern's, Crosthwaite. He preached from the text, 'Ye shall hear of wars and rumours of wars. See that ye be not troubled.'

Keswick received its first practical reminder of the crisis on Monday 3 August 1914, when it became known that all train excursions to the town had been postponed. And at 11pm on Tuesday August 4, Britain declared war on Germany to defend the neutrality of Belgium. Many reckoned the war would be over by Christmas – the 'Hun' rapidly beaten by the gallant British troops with minimal losses.

Corporal Donald James Price who was born in South Wales and served with the Royal Fusiliers (City of London Regiment) from 1914-1920, was on holiday in Keswick on August 4 1914. In an interview with the Imperial War Museum, London in 1988, he said:

> 'Eventually, war broke out and the idea was – I think it was the newspapers who said – you'd better get back to mobilisation. And we went. I remember going to this station. We had go from Keswick and we had to go on a sideline to Lancaster. From there,

Crosthwaite, with St Kentigern's Church/Crosthwaite Parish Church bottom left.

4 THE WESTMORLAND G

THE EUROPEAN CONFLAGRATION.

GERMAN INVASION OF BELGIUM.

A BRITISH ULTIMATUM : WAR DECLARED.

Fighting Begun : Germans Repulsed near Liege.

British Navy Active in the North Sea.

Germany declared war on England at seven o'clock on Tuesday night. No intimation of the declaration was received at our Foreign Office until 10-45 p.m.. On Tuesday morning the British Government dispatched an Ultimatum to Germany. It required that Germany should give an unequivocal assurance that she would respect the neutral territory of Belgium, guar-

numerous proofs of your Majesty's friendship and that of your predecessor, and the friendly attitude of England in 1870 and the proof of friendship you have just given us again, I make a supreme appeal for the diplomatic intervention of your Majesty's Government to safeguard the integrity of Belgium." The reading of this message created a deep impression. Sir Edward Grey suggested that we could not

mines can be fastened round the bulwarks or, on a deck sloping towards the stern, suspended from an overhead tramway. Sometimes they are fastened together with chains or wire hawsers, and matters are so arranged that when put into the water they remain at a depth fixed by the layer. A ship, either an old cruiser, still of good speed, or a fast liner, is fitted in this way, and her business

The European Conflagration: How the *Westmorland Gazette* (which includes news from Keswick) reported the outbreak of war in August 1914.

all these soldiers congregated, all called up, all in uniform – and not in uniforms – and they were on the same train as me and they came down to Manchester and that was the first day.'

On 29 August 1914, posters issued during the day bearing the notices 'What Keswick must do' drew a large gathering to the Keswick market place where a meeting was held relating to the European crisis. A special service of intercession was held in the tiny church at Wythburn near Thirlmere, Keswick, according to the Manchester Evening News on Monday 31 August 1914. The preacher was the Reverend George William Hudson Shaw of St Botolph in London, who lived in Above Derwent in 1891, and in the course of his sermon he referred to the horrors of the war. With outstretched arm, he asked: 'What are you going to do?' An ex-soldier and an employee of the Manchester Corporation Water Works Committee (which undertook the work of Thirlmere) immediately sprang to his feet and exclaimed 'We are going to fight'. The incident deeply moved the congregation. Reverend Shaw married Agnes Josephine Ringrose in Cockermouth in 1890. His only son, Lieutenant Bernard Hudson Shaw, Cheshire Regiment, born in Thornthwaite just outside Keswick, was killed in action by a gas shell on 22 January 1917 and was buried at Berks Cemetery Extension, Hainaut, Belgium.

The Border Regiment (1881-1959) was a line infantry regiment of

Keswick boys and men leaving the town's railway station on 14 September 1914 on their way to fight.

John Peel.

Composer John Woodstock Graves who was born in Wigton, Cumberland, wrote the words for his friend John Peel.

the British Army, which was formed in 1881 under the Childers Reforms by the amalgamation of the 34th (Cumberland) Regiment of Foot and the 55th (Westmorland) Regiment of Foot. 'John Peel' – a hunting melody and battle anthem named after huntsman John Peel, born near Caldbeck – was one of the Border Regiment's quick marches.

On the outbreak of war, the Border Regiment was only five battalions in strength - two Regular, one Reserve (3rd) and two Territorial Force (TF). The 2nd Battalion (Regular) was mobilised for war on 6 October

1914. In its first encounter with the enemy at Kruiseik Hill, Belgium – captured by the Germans on 29 October 1914 and in their hands until 28 September 1918 – the men of the 2nd Battalion were surrounded in their trenches on three sides by the enemy and as a result suffered more than the other battalions fighting in the same battle.

Cap Badge of the Border Regiment.

As the war progressed, the Border Regiment expanded to form sixteen battalions. Six of the regiment's battalions took part in the Battle of the Somme (1 July to 18 November 1916), in which more than one million men were wounded or killed – the long battle of the Somme showed there would be no early or easy victory. Other battle honours include Langemarck, Belgium 1914-17, where the Germans first used poison gas on 22 April 1915 to try and break the stalemate on the Western Front.

According to Cumbria's Museum of Military Life, 6,969 officers and men of the Border Regiment died during the First World War. A further 500 formerly of the Border Regiment lost their lives serving with other units. Of the Border Regiment's war dead, 3,507 are buried with a known grave and an additional 3,462 with no known grave are recorded on memorials to the missing.

Carlisle Castle – Border Regiment off to the War

Members of the Kendal Pals in a captured German trench during the Somme offensive. The photo, taken at Ovillers on 15 July 1916, was a postcard from a series taken by *Daily Mail* photographers.

With conscription politically unpalatable, Lord Kitchener, the newly-appointed Secretary of State for War, decided to raise a new army of volunteers. Men were invited to volunteer with their friends, family and colleagues to form the Pals battalions. The idea was that men were more

A group of Kendal Pals at Bournemouth. Standing – J Ruthven, B Jeffreys, JH Ruthven, WD Walter, E Jeffreys Sitting – E Heatherington, E Tattersall, J Birtwistle, AR Sill, J Proctor.

likely to join up to fight if they did so alongside people they knew, especially in the industrial north. Perhaps the best known and most tragic example of this ill-advised plan is the 11th Battalion of the East Lancashire Regiment, known as the Accrington Pals; 1,000 men who went off to war but only 100 came home. With the introduction of conscription in January 1916, further Pals battalions were not formed.

The 8th (Service) Battalion, Border Regiment (Kendal Pals) was formed in August 1914, and men were recruited in Keswick, Kendal, and Windermere Eight officers and 1,000 or so men were soon assembled. Having completed training, it was time for the 8th Border to move for service overseas. They arrived in France on 27 September 1914. More than 100 Kendal Pals were killed on the Somme according to the Kendal Parish Church archives. The Keswick War Memorial includes twelve Keswick men from the Kendal Pals.

On the day that 'Kaiser Bill', Wilhelm II, visited the Keswick Country House Hotel, on 14 August 1895, he was the main guest of Hugh Cecil Lowther, 5th Earl of Lonsdale, English nobleman and sportsman In the pre-war years, Lord Lonsdale visited Berlin as an Imperial guest. Later, in September 1914, Lord Lonsdale – who had a residence at Lowther Castle, Penrith and inherited huge wealth derived from Cumberland coalmines – would form his own Battalion to fight the Kaiser. When

8TH (SERVICE) BATTALION THE BORDER REGIMENT, 1914-1918

They say we're swanking blighters!

They say we're swanking blighters,
Spick and span, but rarely fighters,
Including officers and all the other ranks.
That we win our fights on paper,
It's the safest blooming caper.
Border swanks!

That we're putty-fisted smiters,
A lot of blatherskiters,
And we're miles behind the Cheshires and the Lancs,
But when it's "Here's your fighting orders"
Just you watch the blooming Borders.
Fighting swanks!

What we practised home in Blighty,
When we did the "High and mighty,"
A-stabbing bags of straw and firing blanks.
We later practised on the Huns
When we took his blooming guns.
Border pranks!

Up at "Wipers" in the mud,
Down at Thiepval sweating blood,
When we went ahead with unprotected flanks.
We were cheerful, though it hurt,
To see our fellows "bite the dirt."
Happy swanks!

Fact, everywhere we've been,
On the Somme or at Messines,
Where we followed up behind a giddy tank,
It was e'er a glorious sight,
To see the Borders fight.
Fight and swank!

Scorching hot, or raining hard,
Vimy Ridge or at Gapaard,
Or evacuated home as "Proud as Yanks."
'Tis still the same old story,
Border lads are England's glory.
Border swanks!
Britain's thanks.

December, 1917.

An 8th Border verse as recalled by Lieutenant-Colonel CWH Birt. Birt, an Australian, was wounded three times during his service, and commanded the battalion later in the war

Lord Lonsdale motored to the Brough Hill Fair, a Gypsy gathering in Westmorland, on 1 October 1917, he was asked by local preacher John Berry what he thought of his friend the Kaiser now. 'The reply was not caught, but it was not lacking in vigour' or so the *Yorkshire Evening Post* of 2 October 1917 reported.

The 11th (Service) Battalion Border Regiment (Lonsdale) – local men drawn from the railways, factories, shops and fields of Cumberland and Westmorland – was formed in Penrith (HQ), Carlisle, Kendal and Workington on 17 September 1914 by the Earl of Lonsdale and an Executive Committee, and Keswick men served with them. Three men were born in Keswick; five enlisted in Keswick, according to the Lonsdale Roll of Honour (ROH). The battalion trained on Blackwell Racecourse on the edge of Carlisle.

The Keswick Country House Hotel, originally owned by the Cockermouth & Penrith Railway, is an elegant Victorian building that is still a hotel.

When Lord Lonsdale was recruiting men for his Lonsdale Battalion, the mayor of Whitehaven, Herbert Wilson Walker, travelled through to Lowther Castle, asking Lonsdale to stop recruiting as it was going to affect coal production. Lonsdale said he was too busy to see Mr Walker, who was mayor between 1913 and 1915, who then had to travel back home. Lord Lonsdale took a great deal of pride in the battalion named after him, paid for their equipment and issued the men with a solid silver hallmarked cap badge. His choice of grey for the uniform was an unfortunate one, as the Kaiser's troops wore that colour. He had already asked the military tailors to buy enough flannel for 1,000 shirts but he was nonetheless overruled and khaki was used here as in the rest of the army

Head and shoulders portrait of Wilhelm II which was presented to Lord Lonsdale by the Kaiser in commemoration of his visit to Lowther Castle in 1895.

In November 1914, St George's Theatre, Kendal showed all week a special local picture filmed at

Blackwell Racecourse, *A Day with the Lonsdale Battalion*. Scenes included physical and company drill, full parade, dinner time, and preparing meals. The Lonsdales did a lot of trench digging there. On 3 January 1915, the Lonsdale battalion had attained a total strength of 1,152 non-commissioned officers and men. By March 1915, it had swelled to 1,350 – the full strength authorised – and on 8 May the Battalion moved to Prees Heath Camp, Shropshire. The battalion would ultimately set sail for France on 23 November 1915.

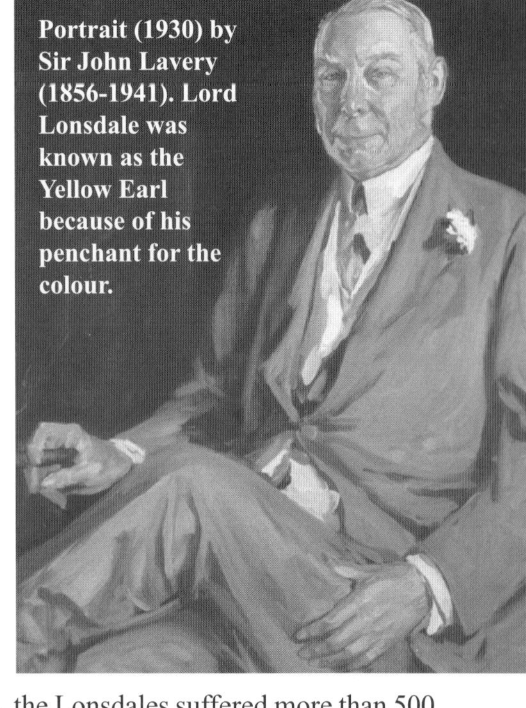

Portrait (1930) by Sir John Lavery (1856-1941). Lord Lonsdale was known as the Yellow Earl because of his penchant for the colour.

On the opening day of the Battle of the Somme, 1 July 1916, the Lonsdales suffered more than 500 casualties out of the 800 who went into action. The commanding officer, Lieutenant-Colonel Percy Wilfred Machell, aged 52, of Crackenthorpe Hall, Appleby, about twenty-five miles from Keswick, was killed on 1 July 1916 at Marne, Champagne-Ardenne while leading his men and is buried at Warloy-Baillon Communal Cemetery Extension. Officers were twice as likely to be killed as the men, largely because they were expected to lead from the front. Percy W Machell is listed on Appleby Cemetery Memorial, a stone obelisk on a four-stepped base, and on Appleby Church Cross.

The Lonsdales spent two years and eight months in France and Flanders. On

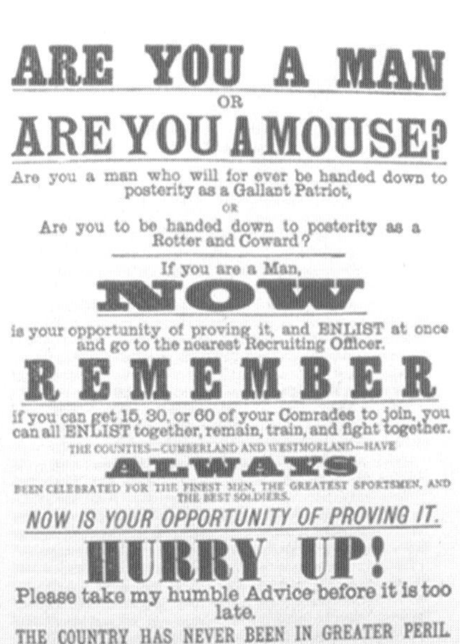

Are You a Man or a Mouse?: The recruiting poster that Lonsdale had printed, said to be a slur on manhood, caused quite a storm. But he said, in September 1914, that he wanted to try and relieve some of the solemnity of some of posters which were out and that he meant nothing derogatory by it.

10 May 1918, the battalion was reduced to basic core strength. On 31 July 1918, it was disbanded. The Lonsdale ROH exists only on the internet (border-regiment-forum.com). It was transcribed exactly as it was printed in HMSO's *Soldiers Died in the Great War*, Volume 39, The Border Regiment.

Lonsdale cap badge: It featured the family (Lowther) crest of a griffin. Apart from the cap badge, the Lonsdale uniform was identical to every other soldier's uniform.

The Lonsdale ROH lists only those who died.

Every year, during both World Wars, Keswick sent a Christmas Gift to all those serving in HM Forces. During World War One, a booklet was included called Keswick's Greetings to her Soldier and Sailor Sons as well as various greetings and messages inside. It also included a list of all 'Keswick's Sons Serving With The Colours'. In the 1917 booklet, these were:

France-225
Italy-11
India & Burma-72
Mesopotamia-19
Palestine-1
Australia-1
Africa-8
Egypt-17
Salonica-33
Malta-1
Gibraltar-1
England-170
Scotland-6
Ireland-11
Navy-18
Prisoners in Germany-6
Missing-13
Discharged Disabled-16
Roll of Honour-58

A total of 687 out of a population of 3,905.

Percy Machell. married Lady Victoria Alice Leopoldine Ada Laura Gleichen in 1905 and they had one son, Roger Victor Machell.

Chapter 2

It was a war of production

As hundreds of men joined up for the Army, their jobs became vacant at home. The two pillars upon which Britain's war effort rested were industry and agriculture. Industry produced the munitions to fight the war, whilst agriculture was vital to produce enough food to fend off starvation as the U-boats took their toll on imports. Farming has been a major industry in the Lake District throughout history, with Herdwick sheep farming being the most common.

The Newlands Valley near Keswick included Threlkeld lead ore and zinc mine which closed in 1926; Brundholme lead mine, which closed in the 1920s; Goldscope lead and copper mine in operation from the 1500s to the end of the nineteenth century; Dale Head copper mine which was started by German miners in Elizabethan times but was closed; Thornthwaite lead mine, closed in 1921; and Force Crag Mine, the last working metal mine in the Lake District, prior to its final abandonment in 1991. Mining was a very dangerous industry. On 6 December 1917, Thomas Bell died from the effects of an accident at Thornthwaite Mines (Keswick Reminder, 5 December 1919). A 1918 inquest into the death of George Dixon, lead miner, ruled that he died at Keswick Cottage Hospital as a result of injuries received in an accident at the Force Crag Mine. The jury said 'the deceased died of incarnation

The Herdwick is a breed of domestic sheep native to the Lake District. *(Lake District National Park).*

of lungs occasioned by being accidentally struck by a piece of metal from a lead mineshot.'

The prosperous period of mining in Elizabethan times was followed later by the manufacture of black-lead pencils made from Borrowdale plumbago. The first record of a factory in Keswick making pencils is from 1832, according to the town's Pencil Museum. The factory left town in 2008, to Lillyhall, Workington.

Barytes-working (barium sulphate) at Force Crag Mine (the High Force Workings), Coledale, above Braithwaite village, dated back to the 1860s, when local men re-opened the lead workings for this mineral. But by 1880, the venture had been given up as uneconomic for price reasons rather than lack of barytes. During the 1914-18 war, Force Crag Mine was worked with some vigour. Barytes ore was extracted for making munitions. At Force Crag Mine, the workforce was increased, the flotation plant and mill were improved and the driving of a major new level was being planned. Despite the fact that mining was such a vital part of the economy of the area, sources vary in the detail of when mines were working and when they closed.

Brundholme lead ore mine (1872-1920) was not worked during the First World War. The Scottish iron and coal masters William Baird & Co abandoned Kelton Fell iron mine, Lamplugh in 1913 and Knockmurton iron mine, Lamplugh in 1914, withdrawing all plant and equipment to its coal interests in Ayrshire, south-west Scotland. The estimated Ayshire output (William Baird) was 1.64 million tons in 1913. Kelton Fell was never worked again, Knockmurton mine closed around 1920, and the Rowrah & Kelton Fell Railway (mineral railway), which was operated by William Baird, closed in 1927.

In 1914, Threlkeld mine employed fifty-four, and Thornthwaite employed eighty, according to Durham Mining Museum. The Honister Slate Mine is the last working slate mine in the UK; quarrying for Westmorland green slate has taken place in the area since 1728. The Honister slate mines reverted to care and maintenance for a while due to labour shortages in the Great War. However, it did not take long for production to recommence after the cessation of hostilities.

John S Birkett, 104th Brigade Royal Field Artillery, eldest son of Isaac and Sarah Birkett (Postlethwaite) of Tithebarn Court, Keswick, worked at Thornthwaite Mine before the war. He enlisted in September 1914, landed in France in June 1915 and was killed by a shell while laying field telephone wires on 16 September 1916. He was buried at Pozieres British Cemetery, north east of Albert, France.

Drill bit and wedge, Carrock Mine. *(Author)*

Private John Peet, 25th (Tyneside Irish) Northumberland Fusiliers, was the eldest son of John and Ann Peet of Henderson's Court, Keswick. Before enlisting in Carlisle, he worked at Thornthwaite Mine and for a time worked in the barytes mines at Ulverston, and for twelve months was engaged in some gold mines in West Africa. He was killed in action on 1 July 1916 (France and Flanders). He is commemorated on the Thiepval Memorial to the Missing of the Somme.

The Germans appreciated the strategic significance of tungsten. The German-owned Cumbrian Mining Company took over Carrock Mine, Caldbeck Fells that produced vital tungsten, in 1904 until the outbreak of the First World War. Under the Defence of the Realm Act (DORA), passed on 8 August 1914 'for securing public safety', the government took increasing control of industry and food production. To meet the wartime demand for tungsten, the Government funded the revival of the mine under the management of mining engineer Anthony Wilson of Thornthwaite, a leading local Liberal who was born in Kendal and who died at Thornthwaite Grange. Tungsten is as dense as gold, has an incredibly high melting point, and is only second in hardness to diamond. These properties made it a vital component in the manufacture of armour plate for ships and machine tools in the munitions industry. The metal was also needed for the filaments of electric light bulbs. Carrock Mine closed in 1919.

Greenside Mine, at the southern end of Ullswater, was a lead mine that during the 1940s became the largest producer of lead ore in the UK. The war years were not uneventful at the mine and accident records

Carrock Fel! Mines, August 2010: With the end of the First World War, government support was withdrawn. *(Mick Garratt)*

show that there were tragedies at home as well as in the theatres of war. In 1914, for example, it is noted that Christopher Temby was accidentally killed by a fall down steps outside the Mine Office. In 1915, board member Henry Winter died, to be replaced by Captain Borlase, who was himself temporarily replaced by his brother when he returned from the front. 1n 1918, William Murray fell into the sump of Skip Shaft and was drowned; smelting at the mine ended.

Wolfram, a tungsten ore. *(Author)*

A German egg bomb – also known as Eier bomb – on display at Cumbria's Museum of Military Life. *(Author)*

Private Ernest Scott Royal Marine Light Infantry, and Private Robert Scott 2nd Border, were sons of Robert and Isabella Scott of Browfoot Brewery House, Keswick. They had been educated at Brigham Grammar school in Keswick. Ernest Scott worked at the Briery Bobbin Mill before enlisting, age 17. He was killed at the Battle of Jutland when HMS *Black Prince* was destroyed by an explosion on 31 May 1916. There were no survivors, all 857 crew being killed. Robert Scott was killed in action (France and Flanders) on 26 October 1917 and is buried at Hooge Crater Cemetery, Belgium.

With the beginning of the war, orders began to flood in at Stott

An example of World War One trench art made by engraving German 77mm shell cases. It reads 'Souvenir of Great War Arras to Lens'. *(Author)*

Derwent Mills: Flax was grown in Ireland which could be shipped to Maryport and then taken by road to Cockermouth.

Park Bobbin Mill, Finsthwaite – 31 miles from Keswick – on Lake Windermere shore for the cotton reels, but also for unusual things such as rungs for rope ladders for the Royal Navy, handles and shafts for the tools to dig the hundreds of miles of new trenches on the Western Front, and for the handles for hand grenades. Trench warfare led to the development of new weapons such as the Stokes trench mortar for high angles of fire which entered service in 1915, and the modification of others such as the Mills bomb hand grenade. The German army developed numerous models of grenade.

'Trench art' is a term used to describe objects made from the debris and by-products of modern warfare. Most trench art was made by servicemen to pass the time when not in the front line. While much of it was simple and amateurish, the production of some examples required metalworking skills or workshop facilities and the men of Keswick, under the influence of Hardwicke Rawnsley and his Keswick School would have probably been particularly adept at this.

The First World War brought prosperity to the flax industry. The Derwent Mills in Cockermouth was founded by Quakers, the Harris family in 1834.The Quakers have long been identified with peace issues and were very involved in domestic matters. It processed flax, a fibre crop, and during the war its main activity was the manufacture of high

The use of parachutes from airplanes was still in its infancy at the outbreak of war.
(The First World War East Sussex)

quality linen fabric for the construction of aeroplane wings and parachutes. There are records of production being taken over by the War Office. During the Great War, Thomas William Harris of Sunnyside, Papcastle, purchased a tank which he presented to Cockermouth. The celebration of a military victory prompted the acceptance of communities of redundant or captured military hardware.

Water from the Lake District had first arrived by gravity in Manchester – 'Cottonopolis' – on 13 October 1894. To members of the Thirlmere Defence Association, who were very much against the plan, there was no question that the preservation of the Lake District was more important than supplying Manchester with the best and cheapest water. City water was still in short supply, as the article headlined 'Hardly a Drop to Drink' in the *Manchester Courier* and *Lancashire General Advertiser* on 18 September 1901 makes very clear. Despite opposition, a second Thirlmere-Manchester pipeline was completed in 1904.

The *Derby Daily Telegraph* published an article published on 23 May 1914 under the headline 'Germans and Thirlmere Aqueduct'. Speaking at Kendal on the subject of home defence, Captain RF Long, recently retired from the 4th Border Regiment (Territorials), said:

> 'The surest way to keep out a foreign foe is to be prepared. At the present time, it has come to my knowledge that one of the first schemes of the Germans is not only to raid this country, but to absolutely cripple us by cutting off the water supplies of our big towns. I met some Germans on the Thirlmere aqueduct at one of the most vulnerable places on it, a couple of miles above Kendal, where the aqueduct crosses the River Kent, and where by a few explosions they could cripple Manchester by cutting off its water supply. It is possible the country does not realise what might result from such tactics, but it is one of the things the Germans are prepared to do in case of the invasion of England.
>
> 'I believe there is work for our Territorials in this connection. They should not only defend our seaports, but also the water

Impounded for the benefit of Manchester: Thirlmere reservoir, at the foot of Helvellyn and feeding the river Derwent, was originally a lake nearly divided into two parts. Over the strait was a picturesque wooden bridge.

> supplies of great centres of population, and I believe Westmorland Territorials could not be better employed than in looking after this great aqueduct which goes through a great deal of wild, unpopulated country from Westmorland to Manchester.'

The *West Cumberland Times* reported on 12 September 1914 that Thirlmere and Keswick waterworks was being guarded by special constables against any possibility of interference, and some of the bridges in the locality were under police supervision. The third of four Thirlmere-Manchester pipe-lines (work had commenced in 1907) was completed in February 1915.

The 'L' Press: Forging the Jacket of an 18-inch gun, Armstrong-Whitworth Works, Openshaw, Manchester. 1918 painting by war artist Anna Airy.

On 27 July 1916, the *Manchester Evening News* reported on preparations for the fourth Thirlmere line. In May 1917, Sir Edward Holt, chairman of Manchester Water Works Committee, said

> 'an extravagant use of water is taking place …It is quite true that there has been a larger consumption for munition works, but apart from this there is every necessity for conserving the supplies.'

A small memorial of local blue slate at Wythburn church, Thirlmere bears the names of Sandham and Bell. *(Ian Stuart Nicholson)*

Many companies switched to making munitions during the war, for example six-inch high explosive shells were produced at the works of the Yorkshire & Lancashire Railway Company at Horwich, Bolton in 1917.

Private Alfred Bell, 11th Border, son of John Bell and Dinah (Weightman), worked for Manchester Corporation Water Works at Thirlmere before the war. He was killed in action at Beaumont-Hamel, northern France on 18 November 1916 and is commemorated on the Thiepval Memorial to the missing and Wythburn Church Memorial on the east bank of Thirlmere. In the shadow of Helvellyn, Wythburn's lonely position attracted the attention of the Romantic Poets. The cottages and inn of the village of Wythburn were drowned when Thirlmere was created in 1894; only the church remains to remind us of the farming village that once existed on this spot. Also commemorated on the Wythburn Church Memorial is Private Joe Sandham, 8th Border. He enlisted at the age of 19 and was killed in action at Mouquet Farm, part of the Battle of the Somme, on 21 October 1916. He was the son of Joseph and Mary Jane Sandham of Helvellyn House, Thirlmere.

The editorial in the *Carlisle Journal* on 9 March 1915 said:

> 'Everyone must admit the need of maintaining the activity of the agricultural industry in time of war, when the question of food supply is of supreme importance, and that any shortage of labour

Fields around Beaumont Hamel after the Battle of the Somme.

> which hinders or curtails the operations of the farm must, if possible, be made good. Even the employment of boy labour ought not be prohibited if no other means of carrying on the work of the farm can be devised.'

There was a large advert in the local press on 16 June 1915 addressed To the Farmers of Cumberland and Westmorland:

> 'The Army Council has decided that in view of the shortage of agricultural labour for the hay harvest, furlough will be given to a limited number of Soldiers of the New Armies and of the Territorial Force for work in the hay harvest as circumstances may permit.'

Furlough is a period of time that a worker or a soldier is allowed to be absent, especially to return temporarily to their own town or country.

For more than 150 years, tourism has been Keswick's principal industry. Many of the impacts of tourism have been positive: jobs for local people; income for the local economy; and increased demand for local food and crafts, for example. The Fabian Society, founded by an Anglian and a Quaker in 1884 in London, was at the forefront of developing political ideas and public policy on the left. The Fabian Society Summer School met at Barrow House in 1914, and 1915, and in Sedbergh (then Westmorland) in 1916 – a different subject was planned for each week. And the Keswick Convention - an annual gathering of evangelical Christians that began in 1875 – met in 1914, 1915, 1916 and 1918. On 21 July 1915, local newspapers carried a letter from Hardwicke Rawnsley:

> '"It has come to my knowledge that some who were intending to come to the Lake District for their holiday have been put off by hearing that in consequence of the war, the holiday makers who would otherwise have gone to the Continent or to the East Coast have thronged the district, and that accommodation is not to be had. I wish to give an emphatic contradiction to the rumour. The scarcity of visitors is felt throughout the Lake Country. Here in Keswick, notwithstanding the Keswick Convention, which commences next Saturday, there are still abundance of rooms procurable."'

The 1915 Convention, according to *The Keswick Story*: The Authorized History of the The Keswick Convention (undated), was wet and so boisterous that the Skiddaw Tent, used to hold Convention, blew down shortly after the Tuesday Bible Reading. The abandonment of the Convention in 1917, owing to the national call to cut travel, came as a blow to the town. To relieve the losses (of the accommodation providers), the Town Council applied to the Government to host convalescent soldiers in the town. Whether they were successful or not is not known. Many villas had been built specially to provide accommodation for well-to-do visitors in 'Convention week'. It resumed in 1918.

The Keswick Agricultural Show, run by the Keswick Agricultural Society and founded in 1860, is traditionally held on August Bank Holiday. It was held on 6 September 1913, according to the *Yorkshire Post and Leeds Intelligencer*, and shorthorn bulls were a strong class. The entries totalled nearly 500 - easily a record number. 26 August 1920 was the first show since 1913 with 'encouraging successes'. 'It was practically a revival of the show, and received sufficient support to ensure a speedy return to its old time success,' according to the *West Cumberland Times* of 28 August 1920.

There was a Herdwick Ram Fair at Keswick in May 1914 (*Yorkshire Post and Leeds Intelligencer*). The Westmorland Agricultural Show and Patterdale Sheep Dog Trials were not held in 1914 owing to the war. The North Lonsdale Agricultural Show was abandoned for 1914 (*Whitehaven News* 13 August 1914). The Penrith Observer of 23 February 1915 reported that Mr JR Robinson of Kirkby Lonsdale proposed that the Westmorland Agricultural Show should be abandoned again, as it was impossible to foretell the end of the war. There was no Agricultural Show in Penrith in 1915 in view of the war. The Grasmere Sports, revived on Wednesday 20 August, 1919, saw a post-war wrestling boom, according to the *Yorkshire Post and Leeds Intelligencer* on 22 August 1919, after a lapse of six years.

The Alhambra Cinema in Keswick stayed open through the war – there are weekly adverts in the *Keswick Reminder*.

Chapter 3

Help on the Home Front

The YMCA was founded by George Williams , a worker in the drapery trade in London. Concerned about the welfare of his fellow workers, he started a prayer and Bible study group. In 1912, the first purpose-built hostels opened in London and Cardiff. During the First World War, YMCA huts were erected with the British Expeditionary Force (BEF), the force sent to the Western Front, at the great bases at Le Havre, Rouen, Calais, Boulogne, Etaples and Abbeville, and subsequently at the frontline. They were a place for rest and refreshments, to read books and newspapers, play billiards or to write letters home using writing paper and envelopes provided by the YMCA. The Keswick branch of the YMCA made appeals for the 'Keswick Hut' – provided and supported by the Keswick branch of the YMCA - in the Calais area, France and for concert parties at the front. The first mention in the *Keswick Reminder* of a YMCA appeal was on 5 November 1915: £100 was needed. On 30 November 1915, £173/3/6 was sent to the front. A YMCA Appeal on 19 January 1916 (Keswick Reminder 4 February 1916) raised £10 to pay

Keswick Hut: The huts were provided to supply a few home comforts to serving troops. *(Cadbury Research Library Special Collections, University of Birmingham)*

for four concerts at the front and a collection for the Keswick YMCA Hut on 6 May 1916 raised £54. It would have been for the use of any servicemen in the area where it was located.

The *Lancashire Evening Post* of Monday 15 July 1918 reported:

> 'Keswick has this week contributed £500 to the YMCA, and £14,000 for the purchase of war weapons.'

With men participating in the war and women in patriotic work, children found their own way to contribute during World War One. In 1912, Keswick & District had three troops (units of scouts) and sixty-five scouts. The following was sent on 6 August 1914 to the editor of the *Carlisle Journal* by Lord Baden-Powell, founder of the Scout Movement.

> 'Hope you can supply about 1,000 Scouts, under District Commissioners, to aid local civic or defence authorities in such duties as collecting or distributing information re supplies, billeting, guarding culverts and telegraph. Assisting Post office, police, fire brigades, ambulance. War office information.'

The Territorial Force (TF) was envisaged as a home defence force for service during wartime. Units were liable to serve anywhere within the UK when the force was embodied, but could not be compelled to serve outside the country. On Sunday 9 August 1914, a telegram was received from Barrow asking that the dress uniforms of the Keswick Territorial Force (TF), then quartered in Barrow might be forwarded. Within half an hour of receipt of the wire, the Keswick Scouts had collected half of the uniforms and had despatched others of their number to Braithwaite, Threlkeld, and Portinscale.

In view of the fear about the presence of spies, particularly ones coming in new-fangled aeroplanes, the deployment of Keswick Boy Scouts in August 1914 was appreciated. The Whitehaven News of 20 August 1914 reported that Keswick Boy Scouts had been stationed on various peaks in the neighbourhood during the past night or two, with sentries stationed on the Greta Bridge and at various points. 'Greta Bridge' related to the still extant bridge at the lower end of Main Street, Keswick, at the western end of the town.

The *Carlisle Journal* on 6 July 1915 reported on the Carlisle Boys 'pioneer training' at Braithwaite:

> 'The Second Carlisle Baden Powell Scouts, under Scoutmaster Lightfoot, were last week in quarters at Braithwaite, where they had the use of a barn belonging to Mr Atkinson, the Royal Oak

Inn. Stuffing their palliasses with straw, they made a shake-down on the floor and took turns in cooking the oats and eggs for breakfast, and the hot-pot or Irish stew and vegetables for dinner. Tea was one essential meal to negotiate and on Sunday a Service at Braithwaite Church was attended, and Bassenthwaite Lake and Coombe Ghyll visited. A long tour was taken on Monday, Force Crag was climbed and the mountain path followed to Buttermere, from whence the road was followed to Honister and then the fells taken for the shortest route to Grange, Swinside and back to Braithwaite.

'Boating on Derwentwater occupied most of Tuesday, and Wednesday was an easy day, bathing and gathering of timber for a bridge over the Braithwaite Beck. This was erected on Thursday, and did the Scouts the utmost credit. When it was completed, it was a bridge of 22ft span, with 3ft roadway and strong enough to break 25cwt. 24 of the Scouts were on it at one time, and it stood their weight without a quiver.

'This pioneer training is one condition of the Scouts' Defence Corps. Mr and Mrs Anthony Wilson entertained the boys at tea at

Buttermere. *(Nick Thorne)*

August 2014: Standard bearers from Keswick Explorer Scouts (they belong to 1st Keswick Scout Group) and Keswick branch of the Royal British Legion stand in silence during the town's commemoration.
(Cumberland and Westmorland Herald)

Middle Ruddings, prior to their departure for home. The same troupe [sic] visited Braithwaite last year and five of that party have now enlisted for the war.'

2nd Lt Todhunter's final resting place.
(Gilbert's Story)

Brigham old boy Second-Lieutenant Gilbert Todhunter, Canadian Infantry, son of George and Margaret Todhunter of 22 Poplar Street, Keswick, was chiefly responsible for the formation of the Boy Scouts in Keswick in 1909. He was the husband of Harriet Todhunter of Kentucky, USA, and was killed in action on 20 May 1915 and is buried at Pont-du-Hem Military Cemetery, north France.

On leaving school, he worked first for Mr Dumble, a picture framer in Borrowdale Road, Keswick. After two years there, he became apprenticed as a carpenter to Charles Clark, a joiner. In 1905 at the age of 15, he joined the Territorial Army (Army Reserve) unit of the Border Regiment. In his capacity as first Scoutmaster, Todhunter welcomed to Keswick on 11 July 1909 a party of twenty German Scouts (under the Wandervogel back-to-nature youth movement) and with his own scouts led the combined troop in procession through Keswick. While in Cheshire visiting his sister Lizzie in 1911, he met Harriet Bebbington from Crewe. Todhunter, Harriet and his other sister Aggie (then working for the Salvation Army in Holywell, North Wales) decided together to emigrate to Canada. They married in May 1912 and set up their marital home in Winnipeg, Canada. He resumed his occupation as a carpenter. The poster featuring Lord Kitchener – Your Country Needs You – was used to encourage recruits to the British & Empire war effort. Canada supported Britain as a member of the Commonwealth under King George V. Todhunter completed an Attestation Paper (a personal information form that volunteers for the Canadian Expedtionary Force completed during the enlistment process throughout the First World War) indicating his readiness to serve at war. His application was for transfer to the regular Canadian Army as a signaller in the Canadian Overseas Expeditionary Force, and he enlisted at Camp Valcartier Quebec in the 10th Infantry Battalion, 106th Winnipeg Light Infantry. He was able to keep his commission, albeit at the lower rank of Second-Lieutenant – again a signalling officer. He commenced training while still in Canada, during which he broke his arm. He transferred to England with the Canadian forces, and they landed on 15 October. By 12 November, Harriet had

Gilbert Todhunter, a Keswick man who died fighting in the Canadian Army.
(Gilbert's Story)

arrived too and went to stay with his mother and Lizzie who by then had moved to Carlisle. His training in England started under canvas on Salisbury Plain and while there he underwent a field officers' course for a major's certificate. He moved on 26 March 1915 to the staging post at Shorncliffe Camp, Folkestone to await orders to travel to France. On 9 April 1915, Harriet came to Folkestone to see him; that would be the last time they would spend together. He and his troop sailed for France on 26 April 1915. From 29 April until 5 May, they were in the trenches. His battalion was heavily involved in the preparation of the battle of Aubers. By the early hours of 10 May, it was over. His troop went into action at Festubert, France on 17 May 1915, and moved during the night of 19 May into trenches previously occupied by the Germans – containing many unburied corpses and unattended wounded men. The 10th Battalion cleared the German redoubt (K5 trench) of enemy for 100 yards, under fire from the enemy, and he was killed. His name appears on both the Keswick War Memorial and the Brigham School memorial plaque.

Gilbert's scouts.

Nearly 1.5 million British men, women and children had emigrated to Canada in the ten years before the war. Of the 458,000 men who joined the Canadian Expeditionary Force from 1914, nearly half were British-born. Private Thomas Forsyth, 28th Canadian Infantry, was killed by a shell. He was a native of Keswick and received his education at Blackman's School and then at Brigham. He was apprenticed to draper John Morley but in 1908 went to Canada.

George and Joseph Blamire, both of the, 8th Border, were sons of Tom and Mary Blamire of High Briery, Keswick. George, who arrived in France in September 1915 and died on 3 July 1916, is commemorated on the Theipval Memorial. For about four years before the outbreak of war, Joseph was a member of the 1st Keswick Scouts. Though only a small-built youth, he persisted in his endeavour to do his bit for his country and volunteered with the big batch of Keswickians who went off in October 1914. He got to France on 25 September 1915, and died of wounds received in action on 22 October 1916. He was buried at Bouzincourt Communal Cemetery north-west of Albert. He had been previously wounded, but only slightly, and returned to the trenches without coming back to England. Joseph was a Brigham old boy and, like his father, worked at the Briery Bobbin Mill prior to the war. *To the*

Sphagnum flexuosum.

Fallen of Keswick contains list of those local men who lost their lives in the First World War. There is no definitive list held centrally and this is why in many cases, numbers of the fallen vary in different sources, with some men being listed more than once, others, not at all.

Throughout the war, 24,598 articles were dispatched from Keswick War Hospital Depot – which closed on 31 March 1919 - plus thousands of bales of sphagnum/bog moss (*Keswick Reminder* 24 January 1919). Millions of wound dressings made from bog moss were used during World War One. Dried sphagnum can absorb up to twenty times its own volume of liquids, such as blood, pus, or antiseptic solution, and promotes antisepsis. Sphagnum was thus superior to inert cotton wool dressings (pure cellulose), the raw material for which was expensive and increasingly being commandeered for the manufacture of explosives.

There are details in the *Keswick Reminder* of Keswick War Hospital Supply Depot equipment sent to hospitals at Liverpool, Carlisle and Colchester on 26 October 1915, to hospitals at Liverpool and the Serbian Depot at London on 1 December 1915, and to Lady Lonsdale's Scheme. Emily, Lady Lonsdale devoted her time to the King George Military Hospital, London, where she went daily to care for injured servicemen. Shortly before her death in 1917, she was working to establish a scheme for the care of paralysed and disabled soldiers near their own homes.

A Grand Patriotic Sale at the Drill Hall, Keswick on 24 November 1915 was held in aid of the local War Hospital Supply Fund/War Working Party. The drill hall is now home to both an outdoor activities hostel business and the Keswick Detachment of the Army Cadet Force. The *Keswick Reminder* of 4 February 1916 gives details of Keswick War Hospital Supply Depot equipment sent to Edinburgh War Hospital and St Johns/Red Cross Societies, London. Equipment was sent to: Liverpool Kirkdale Auxiliary Hospital; Leicester Northern General Hospital; Bristol; Carlisle; Colchester; Edinburgh; Ripon and the French Red Cross at Winchester (*Keswick Reminder* 17 March 1916) and equipment was sent to Ripon Royal Military Hospital; French Red Cross Depot and Liverpool Red Cross Depot (Keswick Reminder 7 April 1916). The Keswick Reminder 23 June 1916 gives details of equipment sent to Liverpool. The Keswick War Hospital Supply Depot received carpet in March 1917 to make ward shoes.

Lady Valda Machell of Crackenthorpe Hall – daughter of the late Admiral HSH Prince Victor of Hohenlohe-Langenburg and Laura Williamina Seymour, and wife of Lieutenant-Colonel Percy Machell, - made a public appeal on 10 March 1915 for:

> 'SOCKS! SOCKS! SOCKS – Will the 1,300 kind friends of the Lonsdale Battalion who so generously responded with mittens at Christmas now add to their kindness by sending them some much-needed socks? (grey preferred).'

On 14 July 1915, Keswick was en fete celebrating the French Flag Day. During the day, little Jonathan Robinson, aged five, dressed in toy admiral costume, and – with a pet hen that followed him everywhere – collected nearly 15s towards a fund for material for making sandbags for the soldiers. Sandbags were invariably used to provide troops with protection at both the front and rear of trenches and were generally stacked some two or three feet deep. Such sandbags – filled with earth by regular filling parties – afforded troops manning the trench fire-step with effective protection from enemy rifle fire. On 15 July the local press carried that week an appeal for thin shirts, socks, cigarettes, writing pads and pencils – or the money to obtain them and other necessary comforts – for the 1st Border Regiment which was then in active service in the Dardanelles. A Keswick Croquet Club tea for the needs of the soldier

Etaples Military Cemetery. Caption: Formerly a vast hospital, the site is now the largest Commonwealth War Cemetery in France.
(Commonwealth War Graves Commission)

boys raised £5/15/- (*Keswick Reminder* 29 October 1915). Cigarettes, known as 'fags', 'gaspers' or 'Woodbines' were not then considered a grave risk to health, but were an essential for many soldiers.

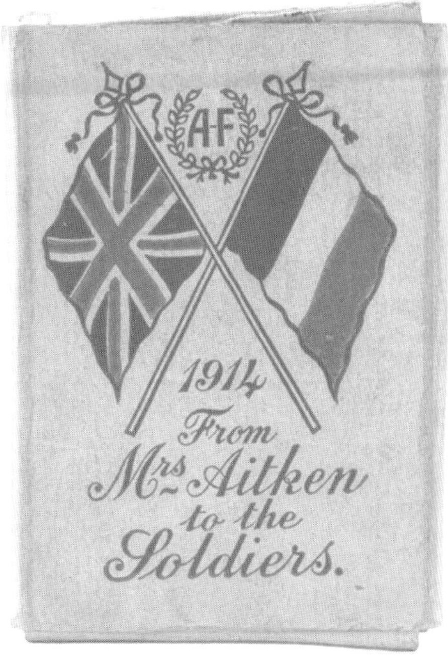

May Aitken, wife of a wealthy Lancashire cotton merchant, sent 10,000 packets of morale-boosting cigarettes to the Front.

During the war, the town of Etaples on the Channel coast, France became a vast Allied military camp and then a 'hospital city'. In November 1915, comforts and magazines were sent to the Keswick bed at the St John Ambulance Brigade Hospital, Etaples, a Base Hospital from July 1915. The Base Hospital was part of the casualty evacuation chain, further back from the front line than the Casualty Clearing Stations. They were manned by troops of the Royal Army Medical Corps, with attached Royal Engineers and men of the Army Service Corps. In the theatre of war in France and Flanders, the British hospitals were generally located near the coast. They needed to be close to a railway line, in order for casualties to arrive (although some also came by canal barge); they also needed to be near a port where men could be evacuated for longer-term treatment in Britain.

Volunteers set up egg collection points to send overseas to hospitals where wounded soldiers and sailors were recuperating. The eggs were packed in sawdust or special boxes and sent to the front. Any that were broken en route were redistributed to hospitals in the UK. The *Keswick Reminder* on 19 January 1917 reported that 18,034 eggs had been sent to Seaforth (Bootle, Merseyside) and Sheffield Hospitals. since April 1915.

There was still a great demand for help on the Home Front in 1919. In a letter dated 16 January 1919 in the Keswick Reminder, M Marshall, Treasurer of Keswick War Relief Committee, said:

> 'I shall be greatly obliged if those ladies who have not returned the work by the end of December for which they had taken out materials and wool during 1918 will kindly send their work to the Girls' Club, Lakes Road on Thursday the 23rd, or 30th of January between 2 and 3-30. This will be a great convenience to the

Sir John Lavery's oil painting (1919) of the war cemetery at Etaples.

committee and thereby save trouble in having to call for it. There is still a great demand for winter comforts for our sailors and soldiers, and we are anxious to send away as much as possible without delay. Since the 1st of January, 120 articles have been despatched to the Countess of Lonsdale's County Depot, to minesweepers, and to the D.G.V.D Com Depot.'

Chapter 4

We will not go to war

In the 19 June 1915 issue of the *Bassenthwaite Parish Magazine*, the Reverend George Kenworthy, born in Barnsley, Vicar of Bassenthwaite from 1895 to 1915 and then Vicar of Pennington, Ulverston from 1915 to 1937, wrote:

> 'We are in for a long serious struggle, and the sooner the selfish shirkers and cowards at home realise this the better. At present a good proportion of the people in the country villages are bent simply upon 'feathering their own nests. Their country may go to perdition for all they care.'

But since there were too few volunteers to fill the ranks, the Military Service Bill was introduced in January 1916, providing for the conscription of single men aged 18-41. In May 1916, the bill was extended to married men and in April 1918 the upper age was raised to 50. Compulsion did not go smoothly. A database of British First World War conscientious objectors (COs) contains material for more than 17,000 men.Very few COs were from Cumberland. Was Cumberland exceptionally patriotic? Perhaps many men who elsewhere might have professed their opposition to the war and to conscription did not do so because they were exempt because of employment regarded as war essential. They kept their heads down. On 5 July 1916, at Penrith, Percy Croysdale Clemenson, 29, clerk, who refused to give his address, was charged with being a deserter from military service.

> 'Prisoner was dressed in what had been a tweed suit of good quality, and his bearing and talk showed that he was of superior social standing,'

So reported the *Nottingham Evening Post* on 6 July 1916. Chief Superintendent Barron said Police-Constable Downing had heard that a strange man was living on the fells of the Helvellyn range between Matterdale and Thirlmere, and when searching the glens on Tuesday he found the prisoner living the life of a hermit in the ruins of an old sheep house by a beck side. He said he had gone there to escape military service, and for ten days had existed on nuts, split peas and oatmeal. He

The Minstrels Gallery (undated), Hawkshead.

was in a very dirty and neglected state. When taken to Penrith, he said he had twice appealed to the Glasgow Tribunals and once to the Central Tribunal and had been refused, and being a CO he had taken refuge in the Cumberland hills. He was remanded for inquiries to be made in Glasgow. Percy Croysdale Clemenson of Edinburgh, The King's (Liverpool) Regiment, formerly Border Regiment, enlisted in Carlisle and is listed as 'Died Theatre of War'. His name is spelt as both Clemenson and Cleminson.

Charles Ernest Marshall (1873-1933) of Derwent Island, Keswick, an orange grower, was over the military service age until 1918 (the upper age was raised from 41 to 50, or 56 if need arose). He served in the Friends' Ambulance Unit (FAU) from 22 October 1915 (Dunkirk) to February 1919 in the Red Cross Section Sanitaire Anglaise. He left France to demobilise on 29 January 1919.

Arthur Frank Pask (1883-1974), of Barrow House, two miles from Keswick, which he managed as a guest house, was a Quaker who served Work of National Importance (WNI) under the FAU General Service (agriculture) from 22 August 1916 at Millbeck House, Keswick, The Nook, Crosby, Maryport, and Carleton Nurseries, Penrith. He was demobilised on 21 December 1918.. He died in 1974 in Lincolnshire.

An example of a local CO who put his head above the parapet was Frederick William Scott, aged 28, a school master at Workington Technical College. He failed to report on 5 April 1917, was fined 40/-

and handed over to Military. He had the guts to stand up in court and say he was a CO. After arrest and trial he was sent to Carlisle and forcibly enlisted in the 3rd Battalion of the Border Regiment. He refused to obey orders, was Court Martialled at Litherland on 24 April 1917 and sentenced to one year with hard labour. He continued to disobey orders and between April 1917 and April 1918 was Court Martialled on two more occasions. He served his sentences in Wormwood Scrubs and Walton prison, Liverpool. He refused to accept any of the government schemes for COs and was among the 1500 men known as 'Absolutists'. Having become ill while in Walton prison, he was released in January 1919. The illness had rendered him stone deaf.

Of eight 'absentees' and 'deserters' reported in the *Whitehaven News* in 1915, 1916 and 1917 (they were not described as COs) is Thomas Park. He had appeared at Whitehaven Magistrates Court and was on remand having failed to report for military service (Whitehaven News, 20 September 1917). He was from Mosser, Cockermouth and ended up serving in the FAU, founded by the Quakers – many of those who became known as COs were Quakers. FAU members were trained at Jordans, a hamlet in Buckinghamshire. Altogether, it sent more than 1,000 men to France and Belgium, where they worked on ambulance convoys and ambulance trains with the French and British armies. The FAU continued to operate throughout the duration of the First World War.

On 27 August 1915, a lecture at the Fabian Society Summer School was given by Mr H Suell entitled Imperial Eugenics. He said he was quite prepared to see something like a human strike instead of an industrial strike brought to bear on the governors of nations, unless they could arrange that international life should no longer be the plaything of diplomats and intriguers.

Following the Great War, the parents of the historian AJP Taylor, Percy Lees Taylor and Constance/Connie, either owned or rented a holiday cottage in Hawkshead, a South Lakeland tourist honeypot seventeen miles from Keswick. In the summer of 1919, the Taylors gave holidays to a stream of COs newly released from prison and selected by Preston solicitor William Henry (Harry) Thompson who was imprisoned as a CO. Harry was Connie's brother and the cottage was the Minstrel's Gallery, Berkeley Square, Hawkshead.

Catherine Elizabeth Marshall and her parents lived at Hawse End, Keswick. She and her mother joined the National Union of Women's Suffrage Societies (NUWSS) and established a branch in Keswick. In 1911, the NUWSS had enough funds to appoint Catherine Marshall and

Catherine Elizabeth Marshall.

Kathleen Courtney to full-time posts at national headquarters. In July 1914, the NUWSS argued that Asquith's government should do everything possible to avoid a European war. Although the NUWSS supported the war effort, it did not follow the Women's Social and Political Union's (WSPU) strategy of becoming involved in persuading young men to join the armed forces. In April 1915, Marshall joined the Women's International League for Peace and Freedom (WILPF). The No-Conscription Fellowship (NCF) also received support from Marshall. She fell in love with Clifford Allen, the chairman of the NCF, who was imprisoned in 1916. Unwilling to co-operate with the prison authorities, Allen was placed in solitary confinement and put on a diet of bread and water. Suffering from tuberculosis and close to death, he was released in December 1917.

Chapter 5

Inspirational women

Stories of the Great War tend to focus on men. It takes a great deal of effort to see past the servicemen to the women, who have their own wartime stories.

Constance Lilian Louise Highton was born in Workington in 1898 (1911 Census), the daughter of the first headmaster of Brigham School, Robert Ernest Highton and there is a window in memory of her at Keswick St John. Her father was headmaster from 1880 to 1907 and superintendent of the Brigham Sunday School. She was a VAD (member of the Voluntary Aid Detachment) nurse in the war and died, aged 20, in late 1918 at St George's Hospital, London of Spanish flu. She was educated, as a boarder, at Calder Girls School, Seascale. Her memorial is a stained glass window by Powell of Whitefriars.

It was reported in the *West Cumberland Times* on 30 November 1918:

> 'Deep regret and sympathy with the bereaved parents were felt when it became known that Miss Constance Lilian Louise Highton, younger daughter of Mr & Mrs RE Highton, Newlands, Workington had died in London after a brief illness. For the past two years Miss Highton had been engaged in VAD work in London hospitals. About three weeks ago she was taken ill with influenza, which was followed by pneumonia and other complications, death taking place on the 18th inst at the early age of 20 years. Of a sympathetic, patient and loving nature, Miss Highton was eminently fitted for the work she undertook, in which she showed zeal and efficiency, combined with a kindliness which gained her the esteem and affection of the sick to whom she administered, as well as her fellow-workers...'

[Her brothers were Major Langton Highton and Lieut-Commander Mark Highton RN. Amongst the mourners were representatives from the Cadogan Square Hospital for Officers, the Seely VAD Hospital of 30 Princes Gate and the Professional Classes Hospital, Princes Gate]

Nursing sister Florence Mary Anderson, Canadian Army Medical Corps, of Ontario, Canada, married at Keswick St John's on 22 December 1917 and the event was reported in the Keswick Reminder on

Highton window: Locally it is known as the Resurrection Window. The top lights show Mary Magdalen and Mary, mother of Jesus bringing spices to anoint His body. The bottom lights show Florence Nightingale and Dorcas tending the sick and clothing the needy.

4 January 1918. She emigrated to Canada in 1910 (the passenger ship RMS *Saxonia* arrived in Massachusetts, USA and then border crossings were made to Canada).

Lord and Lady Rochdale converted their Keswick home, Lingholm on the shores of Derwentwater, into a VAD hospital. Lingholm Military Hospital in Portinscale, an auxiliary hospital, opened on 4 May 1917. The patients at auxiliary hospitals were generally less seriously wounded than at other hospitals and they needed to convalesce. Cash and gifts were given to the hospital and equipment loaned to the hospital. On 29 May 1917, a Primrose League Flag Day for Lingholm Hospital and Hostels for Sailors and Soldiers Suffering from Nerve Strain raised £24. Private William Shaw Gash, who was born in Keswick, was a gardener on Lord Rochdale's Keswick estates. He was not yet twenty when awarded the Military Medal for distinguished conduct and bravery on the field.

On 26 September 1917, Lingholm Military Hospital had twenty-six beds for officers, and sixty-seven men had been treated there since 7 May 1917. In the rest of 1917, thirty-three officers were treated, then 112 in 1918 and twenty-five in 1919 before closure on 30 April 1919 with a closing balance of funds of £346/18/8d.

One page of the autograph book reads:

'Thanks is but a little word
To put in this little book/
But with an honest meaning
how BIG THE WORD CAN LOOK.
Thanks. T.R. Williamson, 10th Sherwood
Foresters.'

Clara Cockbain of St John's Street, Keswick, served as a VAD at Lingholm Military Hospital. She was a member of the old Keswick family of Birkett Cockbain, and brother of William Birkett Cockbain, holder of the Military Cross. She was a

A VAD uniform.

Lingholm, which was built in the 1870s. *(Lingholm Estate)*

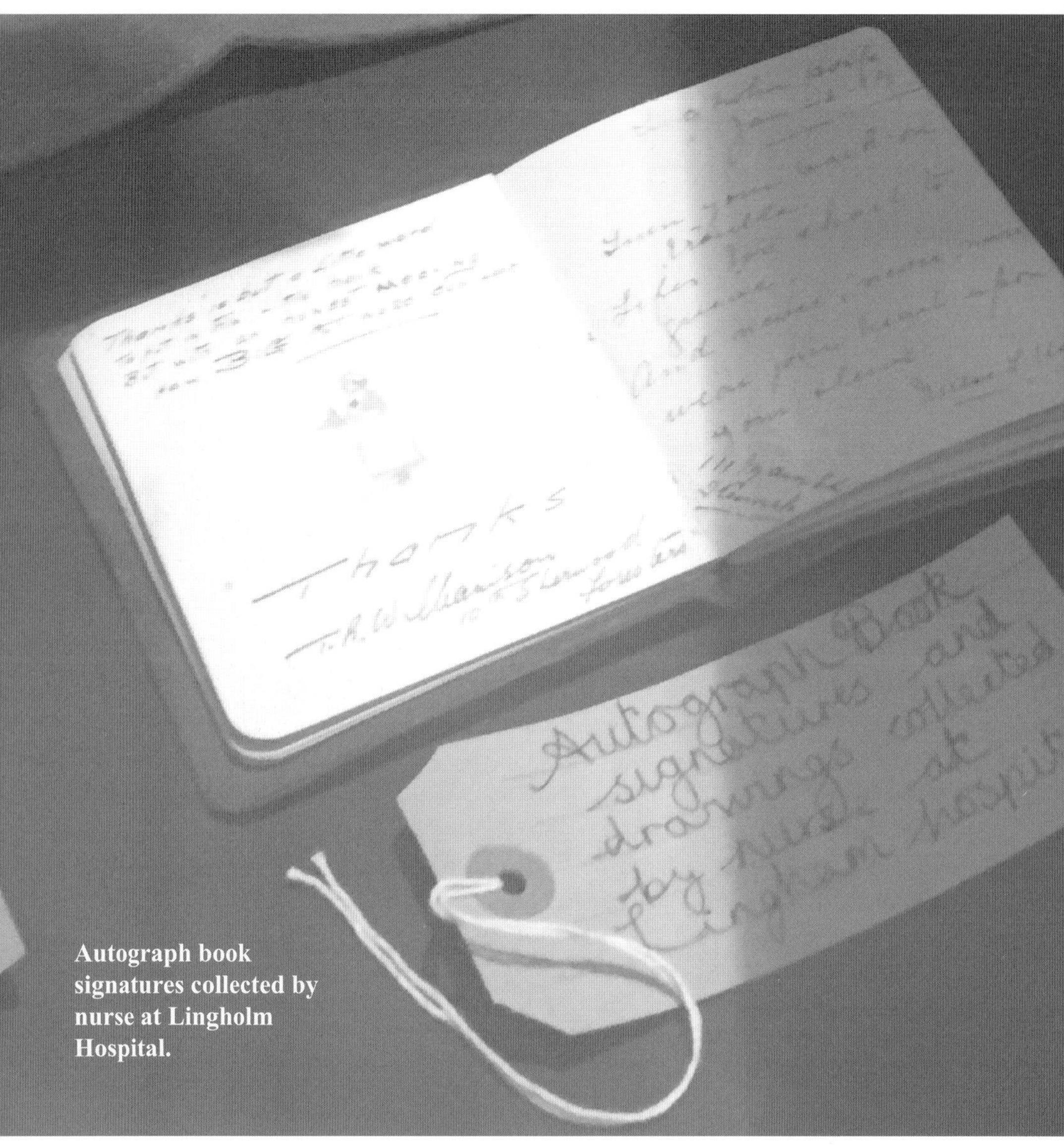

Autograph book signatures collected by nurse at Lingholm Hospital.

chemist in 1911 and carried on the butchery business established by her husband Ernest.

Keswick names feature strongly on the strength of volunteers and staff at auxiliary hospitals in Cumberland: Dora Brown of Keswick; Lily Clark of Keswick; Dorothy Furnace of Crosthwaite; Lizzie Furnace of Crosthwaite; Edith Jacques of Threlkeld; and Jane Johnstone of Keswick. Rita Johnstone, Dinah O'Connor and Hilda Rathbone worked

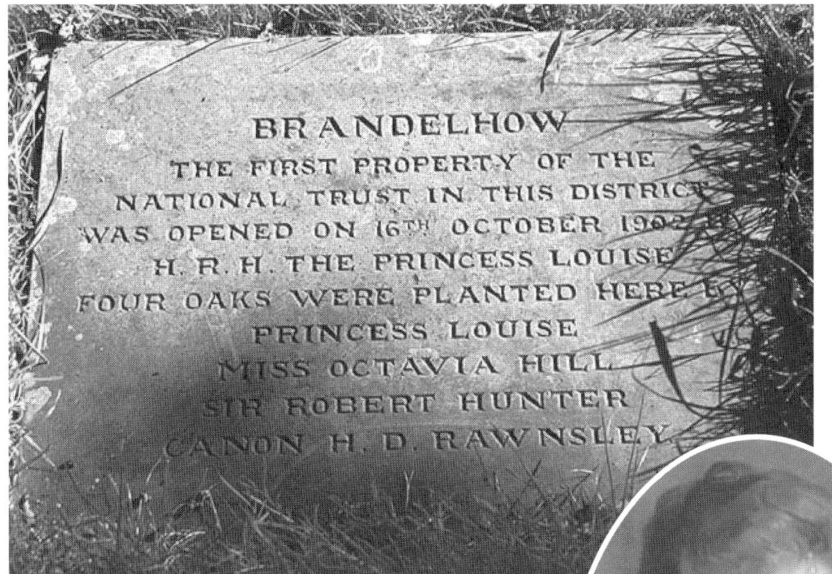

Commemorative stone: Brandlehow. Four oaks were planted here by Princess Louise, Rawnsley and co-founders of the NT Octavia Hill and Sir Robert Hunter. *(Visit Cumbria online)*

as VAD nurses at Lingholm Military Hospital. There were 27 auxiliary hospitals in Cumberland during the First World War. These included Cockermouth Castle and Bankfield Mansion, Workington. Mr Appleton of Cockermouth, Dr Atkinson, Arthur Bell of Cockermouth, Mr Fawcett and J Grave worked there on a voluntary basis.

Princess Louise was the sixth child and fourth daughter of Queen Victoria and Prince Albert.

Lucy Eleanor Jolley (1870-1943) of Lorton had just been appointed as Matron-in-Chief of the Independent Air Force after a brilliant nursing career, according to the Daily Mirror of 3 July 1918. Miss Jolley, who received her training at Guy's Hospital, London, was appointed matron of the Royal Southern Hospital, Liverpool on 15 September 1910. The Independent Air Force was a strategic bombing force which was part of the RAF and used to strike against German railways, aerodromes and industrial centres without co-ordination with the Army or Navy. Miss Jolley, who had three brothers and one sister, died in Surrey in 1943 (no known children).

If he were asked for a description of what the position ought to be in English agriculture that summer (1916), said Mr Acland at the annual meeting of the Women's Farm and Garden Union (WFGA) he should modify and adapt the well-known lines of Macaulay (a British historian and Whig politician) as follows:

The harvest of East Anglia
This year old maids must reap
This year young boys in Cumberland
Must dip the struggling sheep.
And in the pails of Lunesdale
This year the milk must foam
From the white hands of strapping girls
Whose aires are gone from home.

The WFGA was the most important of the bodies which had dealt with women's work on the land before the war. The Women's Land Army (WLA) was established in February 1917, and was affectionately known as the Land Girls. It recruited, trained and placed thousands of women in Britain's farms. There were three sections to the WLA: agriculture; forage (haymaking for food for horses); timber cutting. The majority who worked in agriculture were milkers and field workers. In April 1917, enthusiastic and well-educated young women were chosen to become 'Gang Leaders'. These women had to take responsibility for the work of three to-four fields workers who worked as 'land girl gangs' on individual farms from June to October each year. The WLA was disbanded in 1919. Some members continued on the land, some falling in love with and marrying farmers or becoming farmers themselves. This romanticised version was perhaps appropriate in the immediacy of the return to peace.

The memorial tapestry inside St Herbert's Church, Braithwaite names nine men and one woman, Sarah Barnes, sister of Caleb Barnes, who later became the very beloved headmaster of Braithwaite primary

WLA band worn by Madge Richardson of Thursby near Carlisle.

Herbert Barnes who married Frances Wilson in 1894.

school. She was born in Braithwaite and served in the WLA, working on a farm at Burgh-by-Sands, Carlisle. While at the farm, she contracted influenza, which developed into pneumonia. She died at the age of 19 on 12 March 1919.

For years, girls who were brought up to farm work had been leaving the land and migrating into the large towns to fill positions as domestic servants – a luxury for the well-to-do people in the large towns. The Cumberland Guild of Agricultural Workers, another organisation dedicated to helping the war effort, aimed to recruit town girls to work on farms during the busy spring and summer periods. Lads too young to join up were also targeted. The intention was to bus these volunteers, in groups, from the town to the outlying farms where they would spend their weekends working in teams.

Author Beatrix Potter, who as a farmer and landowner came to experience the changes the war brought to rural life in Britain, spent nine summers at the Lingholm Estate between 1885 and 1907. In 1910, she campaigned against working horses being conscripted, if war broke out. 'No doubt we should be paid for our horses,' she wrote in a leaflet titled The Shortage of Horses, 'but what about our ruined crops?' One million horses were sent to France to fight in the Great War and only 62,000 came back. Horses pulled guns, ration carts and ambulances by day and night, often in terrible conditions. An advert on page one of The *Daily Telegraph* on 13 February 1915 by the Purple Cross Service calls for donations to relieve the suffering of war horses. On 18 May 1915, in a letter to Harold Warne, her editor, Potter said: 'I do hope your nephews are all alive and unhurt – or not badly. Sometimes it is a relief to have them safe in hospital.' Her nephew, Second Lieutenant Hilary Loraine Heelis joined the army on 1 June 1916 as a private soldier, giving his prior occupation as 'school lad'. He

Recruitment poster for the WLA, 1917.

Beatrix Potter and Hardwicke Rawnsley, who encouraged her to publish The Tale of Peter Rabbit. *(National Trust)*

became an officer with the Lancashire Fusiliers in 1917 and was taken prisoner in France on 4 June 1918 during a trench raid when the Germans captured Veuilly-la-Porte. He returned to Britain and died, aged 40, in Bolton, Lancashire. Beatrix Potter lost a distant set of cousins when the passenger liner Lusitania was torpedoed by a U-boat off the southern coast of Ireland on 7 May 1915.

In 1916, she wrote to *The Times* about the shortage of labour on small farms in wartime. As a result of this letter, Eleanor Louisa (Louie) Choyce – who had been the governess to a wealthy family in Gloucestershire – went to work for her. Her investment was, as it turned out, in a farming friendship which would last the rest of her life. Hill Top Farm near Hawkshead, bought by Potter in 1906, now boasted a sizeable flock of chickens, turkeys and some ducks which produced income but also provided food on the farm. Rationing and wartime shortages meant that even rabbits were raised as farm stock. Potter, best remembered for her books such as *The Tale of Peter Rabbit,* confessed she did not like having them killed. Peter Rabbit featured in a poster produced by Potter as part of a campaign calling for a restriction on the import of German goods in 1910, after she found herself unable to get a local business to manufacture Peter Rabbit dolls for her, as the market had already been flooded with cheap, unauthorised imports from Germany.

On 18 May 1915, Lord Kitchener in the House of Lords insisted on the importance of an adequate supply of munitions. Construction work on Gretna munitions works started in November 1915. The *Keswick Reminder* reported on 5 October 1916 that women and girls over 16 were wanted to work there HM Factory Gretna produced cordite – the propellant for shells – for the British Army. By 1917, the larger proportion of the workforce were women: 11,576 women to 5,066 men

A number of Keswick women worked at Gretna munitions works and they are listed in the *Keswick Reminder* soldier index from 30 July 1915 to 8 November 1918 and from 10 January 1919 to 31 December 1924., They include Elizabeth Hogg and her sister Alice, both of 11 Derwent Street, Keswick (1911). They lodged there in hostels, rather than travelling daily. Munitions worker Annie Fulton of Park Holme, Keswick left by train to live at Gretna (*Keswick Reminder* 20 October 1916). Keswick munitions workers who lived at Gretna also include: Agnes Ellen Bainbridge of Ratcliffe Place; Ellen Banks and Agnes Annie Chapman of Leonard Street; Mona Maud Cowley of Poplar Street; Florence Jane Hayton of West View; Sarah Ann Parker of Lydias Cottages, Brigham; Grace Robinson of Lake Road, Keswick; Mary Ann Stewart of Gatey's Court; Maggie Thomason of Derwent Street; Ella Jane Thompson of Ratcliffe Place; Sarah Thompson of Derwentwater Place; Jane Tiskell of Braithwaite; Annie White of Southey Street, Keswick; and Ellen Woof of Poplar Street,

The Ministry of Munitions made as much use as possible of workers not needed for the Army – the old, the young and women. According to a list of National Factories Controlled by the Ministry of Munitions, 1915-1918 compiled by Birmingham University, the Workington National Shell Factory was in Stanley Street. It was a national projectile factory controlled by the Ministry of Munitions. All lots were cleared by 8 February 1919, when the site was handed over to Hudson, Scott & Sons of Carlisle to open a mechanical toy factory. Miss James, who was forewoman of the shell factory, was appointed manager of the new factory, in charge of 200 girls.

The *Workington Star* on 13 April 1917 reports on a football match between the Munition Girls of Workington and Carlisle, with the team members named.

The East Cumberland Shell Factory in Carlisle was at the Drill Hall in Strand Road and had a largely female workforce. On 5 July 1915, the recent issue of the *Carlisle Diocesan Gazette* said that several of the clergy in the Diocese had offered themselves for service either as chauffeurs or as makers of shells.

> 'These latter will work at making shells from Monday to Saturday, and on Sunday will return to their parishes for Sunday duty.'

On 16 September 1915, Aspatria Station had the honour of having the first lady clerk to be employed on the Maryport & Carlisle Railway. The attempt to replace the office staff there who have enlisted with youths had not been successful. The experiment of a young lady clerk was therefore being tried. On 19 September 1915, girl telegraph messengers were the latest innovations at Keswick.

The 12 September 1915 issue of the *Carlisle Journal* advised women:

> 'it is to be hoped that fantastic, unmeaning and frivolous dressing will be abandoned for more womanly fashions. The serious pursuits women are engaged in now, the voluntary service given by our sex to the State, and the grave aspect of our national affairs in general, not to mention the dread toll of young life paid, must naturally in all but the most frivolous and unfeeling, produce an attitude of mild repellent of folly and extravagance in any form, dress included.'

In the *Carlisle Journal* on 3 October 1915, Muriel in Our Ladies Budget wrote:

> I see already that some advanced followers of Fashion are attempting the swinging gate of kilted men, their full skirts swaying about the knees in unison. The vanity and folly of it are deplorable. I heard in the streets the following remarks from two working men "There ain't no womanly women now". A mounted policewoman riding astride her horse provoked this disparaging comment. Stern necessity at the present time forces women to do some of men's work and this inevitably brings about a change in their manners and deportment."

According to the *Keswick Reminder* on 24 January 1919, Alice Cowperthwaite was the Honorary Secretary of the Comrades of the Great War (Women's Section). Those eligible for membership were wives, mothers, sisters, widows and daughters of comrades. The Comrades of the Great War were formed in 1917 as a non-political association to represent the rights of ex-servicemen and women who had served or had been discharged from service. The Women's Section formed an autonomous section within the 'Comrades' and this tradition continued after the formation of the British Legion in 1921.

Chapter 6

Belgian refugees

Britain declared war on Germany on 4 August 1914 when the latter invaded neutral Belgium. Early in October 1914, a large party of Belgian refugees arrived at Kendal where a crowd of an estimated 3,000 people had assembled to give them a rousing reception. They were looked after in four hostels under the banner name 'Belgian Settlement for Kendal and District' with the treasurer Issac Braithwaite; each was looked after by a matron and a stores/housekeeping committee. The hostels were called Prospect, Castle Mount, Holly Croft and Silverhow (all on Kendal Green). The driving force behind the settlement was Arthur Simpson, the head of a wood carving business in Kendal, and Jane Simpson (nee Davidson), both Quakers. They had a daughter Hilda who worked as a home assistant in 1911. Jane Simpson, who was born in Monaghan, Ireland, was awarded the Belgian Medaille de la Reine Elizabeth for assistance to refugees. And in the summer of 1918, Mary Farish Brown of Lowther Street, Whitehaven was awarded the Gold Medaille de la Reine Elizabeth for similar service

On 16 October 1914, the *Carlisle Journal* reported that a family of Belgian refugees from Mailines had arrived at Penrith. The family was offered hospitality by a Mr and Mrs Wainwright. The Belgian family consisted of a father, mother, daughter and son. They were described as respectable tradespeople and they had lost all their possessions, except the clothing they stood in.

At Workington Hippdrome, there was a sacred concert on 18 October 1914 in aid of the general relief effort. On the same day, there was a sacred concert at Keswick, held on behalf of the 'Belgian and local relief funds'; the admission by silver collection raised £10.The Key Brothers orchestra played overtures; Miss Ward of Braithwaite wore a sash of Belgian colours to give a recital of an Austrian war incident; Miss Usher sang two solos; Mrs G.A Wilson rendered 'Abide with me' and 'Land of Hope and Glory' as solos; Frank Dobie of Workington displayed his fine voice in two poems and the quartette party overcame the audience with their sheer musical ability. There was a dramatic finale with the singing of the National Anthem by a number of Keswick Territorials.

On 22 October, a refugee family had arrived at Rothay Manor, Ambleside; Joseph Burseniers (a master builder), his wife Louise and son Marchel Abta with his wife of three months Juliette, had arrived via the Ostend to Folkestone boat. The first refugees arrived at Whitehaven on 27 October 1914. The Whitehaven Colliery Company had paid for their train fares from London and was going to provide work for them at Ladysmith Pit.

On 5 November 1914, there were already fifty-seven refugees in the Penrith area, ten at Maryport and twenty-nine at Workington, with promises of space for fifty at Alston, thirty at Whitehaven and forty at Keswick, with arrangements ongoing at Longtown, Brampton, Cockermouth and Wigton. On 9 November 1914, five Herdwick lambs were sold several times over at Mitchell's mart, Cockermouth to raise £114 for Belgian relief. Similar events happened at Workington Mart on 11 November 1914 and Millom Mart on 16 November 1914.

Rickerby House, Carlisle was sold in July 1914 to Mason Thompson Scott, a director of a building company, owner of the Crown & Mitre in the city and rugby international, for £7,000. Not wishing to live there himself, Scott offered Rickerby House in October 1914 to the relief committee for Belgian refugees set up by Tavistock, in Devon, in October 1914. On 26 November 1914, forty-four Belgian refugees arrived at Carlisle station and were taken to Rickerby House,, the number rising to forty-nine in December. This was a holding centre before accommodation could be found for them elsewhere. Refugees at Rickerby House wore labels on their breasts and on the whole they were people of the better middle classes. Meanwhile, other houses in Carlisle were acquired on loan and citizens lent their furniture. Belgian children attended Carlisle schools. In March 1915, it was stated in the *Carlisle Journal* that Rickerby House would have been empty if Belgians were not there.

On 23 November 1914, six refugees arrived at The Cross, Hensingham. The Cross had room for many more refugees. These families were Roman Catholic and attended the RC School. By 18 December, twelve more had arrived and a married couple and their child were staying with Mrs Moore at Cartgate. The plan was for the men of this second party to work making munitions at Workington.

An article in the *Penrith Observer* on 2 March 1915 reported on a scheme devised by James Watt to provide work on farms for Belgian refugees. It had come to an end. An enormous majority of the men who have come to Great Britain from Belgium seem to have been

KESWICK.

Blencathra Hotel,

KESWICK.

Temperance and Commercial

JOSEPH MILLER, Proprietor.

Comfortable Dining, Drawing, Sitting, and Smoke Rooms. Good Bedrooms.

TERMS, TARIFF, Etc., ON APPLICATION.
Special Terms for Families and Parties.

Daily Coaches

From the Hotel to Ambleside, Windermere, Buttermere, and during the Season.

Keswick inset 1

1906 *Guide to Keswick and its Vicinity* in the *Penny Guide Books* series, published by Abel Heywood and Son, Manchester, and by Simpkin, Marshall, Hamilton, Kent and Co of London.

accustomed to occupations other than agriculture. It would be as unreasonable to expect these to be able to adapt themselves to rural occupations as it would be to suppose that Lancashire operatives could

DERWENTWATER LAKE,
NELSON'S "BLENCATHRA"
Family & Commercial Temperance Hotel,
(OPPOSITE THE WESLEYAN CHAPEL),
SOUTHEY STREET, KESWICK.

Five minutes' walk from the Station. Pleasantly situated, commanding extensive Mountain Scenery. Recently enlarged and re-furnished. A Ladies' Drawing Room. Hot and Cold Baths. Posting in all its Branches. A 'Bus meets all trains.

G. M. NELSON, (late John H. Jeffery,) Proprietor.

Nelson's Blencathra was on Southey Street and opposite the Wesleyan Chapel, and five minutes' walk from the station.

do a similar emergency turn to the work of a Cumberland fellside farm. A number of refugees – seemingly two families – stayed in apartments at the Blencathra Temperance Hotel, Keswick, also known as Nelson's Blencathra. In 1906, Joseph Miller was innkeeper. There were also about twenty-three refugees at Cockermouth. The *Keswick Reminder* reported on 10 December 1915 that the Keswick Belgian Committee was set to dismantle the Blencathra Hotel in Keswick. This appears to mean that the hotel had been set up as a refugee centre but was not now needed.

By 13 March 1915, refugees were getting work in all kinds of sectors, for example, Op de Beeck who was employed with the LNWR (London North Western Railway) at Carlisle on 23/- per week. On 4 October 1915, de Beeck and his family moved to Workington where he had obtained work at the Steelworks. Francois Dralaus was to work as a barber and shaver at the Wordsworth Street School, Penrith and Skiddaw Grove, Penrith VAD Hospitals.

On 14 August 1915, Charles Speler appeared at Keswick Court on charges of being drunk and of infringing the Aliens Registration Act, which had come into force immediately war had been declared. Anyone not a British citizen was required to register with their local police and also demonstrate that they were of good character and that they had a good command of English – this was considered to be an effective way to reduce the risk of spies. Speler was working as a journeyman painter at Workington earning 33/- per week and with a war disablement pension of 14/- per week. He was fined 5/- and £2 respectively for the two offences.

On 4 October 1915, Jean Francois Frenay, 50, of Barnes Lane, Workington was killed by a rock-fall while haggling coal in the 'lying position' at the Main Band seam of Lowca No 10 colliery at around 8am. He had worked at Milmort Colliery, Belgium before the war and had worked at Lowca for three or four months.

A Belgian marriage took place at Maryport on 25 September 1915. The parties were Clarence De Weerdt, Belgian House, Harrington, and Clementine Van Makot of Collins Terrace, Grasslot. The groom was employed on munitions work under the Workington Iron and Steel Company and the bride had been among the first party of Belgian refugees that had come to Maryport about eleven months earlier. The ceremony was performed by Father Dupont, from Ypres, Belgian chaplain for the district, now in residence with Father Fishwick in Cockermouth.

On 28 August 1916, a Belgian miner, Theophile Wustenberg living at Northside, Workington, was killed by a rock fall in the Main Band seam of Lowca N° 10 Pit. The fall knocked him over, crushed his head and broke his neck – death was instantaneous.

On 14 March 1919, the Keswick Reminder printed a letter of thanks from Belgian refugees M and Mme Breugimans, now returned to Antwerp. A formal letter of thanks for the hospitality of the United Kingdom to the refugees was sent in August 1919 from His Excellency Monsieur le Baron de Brocqueville, Minister of the Interior for Belgium. Millom coped with a massive influx of Belgian refugees. In April 1915, it was noted that there were 640 workmen, mainly Belgians, travelling to Vickers shipyard in Barrow every day. A Belgian lady teacher arrived in Millom on 29 July 1915 and taught at St James' Roman Catholic School.

The *Above-Derwent Newsletter* on 14 June 1916 reported that Victor Van de Paar, the Belgian who found a home in Braithwaite, has been needed by his Government: 'It rather looks as if the Belgian Railways were going to get work again. He has been very happy here. As he was called away very suddenly, he wishes to express his warm thanks for all the kindness he has received whilst here.'

In all, 72 Belgians lived in the Penrith area for various periods of the war. During their stay, they had free entrance to the Alhambra cinema, and also honorary membership of various clubs in the town, free medical care by Dr Erdington and free dental treatment by Mr J Morton.

A Belgian refugee, Suffragette Madame Roberts (nee Eveline Chapelle), the wife of the marechal des logis, Chief General de Gendarmerie Belgique (marechal des logis was the equivalent of a sergeant in a cavalry or artillery regiment), disappeared mysteriously. She had homes at Woodmansterne in Sussex/Surrey and in the Keswick area. A lot of mystery remains in the story, such as what happened to her for two months and quite how she got from London to Buxton untraced and in wartime conditions. She vanished between the Alexandra Palace reception centre and her placement lodgings at Peterborough in October 1914, while she was heavily pregnant. After a long search she was eventually found with family friends in early January 1915 at Errwood Hall, Buxton, Derbyshire when she was almost due to give birth.. She was said to be in a very confused state after her flight from Belgium and fearful that she had lost her husband in all the confusion. She had arrived there on 18 December 1914 in a 'delicate state of health'. Her husband was later traced at Dunkirk.

Chapter 7

Prisoners of War in Germany

If you were in Germany on holiday at the outbreak of war then you were arrested as a prisoner of war. Workington has two examples, one of which was the Rector of St Michael's Church the Rev Curwen. People were released two or three months later if they were just holiday-makers. The *West Cumberland Times* reported on 8 September 1914 that the Rector S.P.L. Curwen of Workington was holidaying in Germany when the war broke out and had since been detained. The letter was written in Bavaria and brought to England and posted by a lady family friend, as English women and children were allowed to leave the country.

In February and March of 1915, the first batch of permanently disabled British prisoners arrived home. Those who had been in Germany were unanimous in their assertions that the British prisoner was selected for worse treatment than the Belgian and the French. They complained of lack of food and clothing (*Daily Telegraph*, 18 February 1915). The German government was making prisoners work on the land and in coal mines, contrary to the Hague Convention. There were no doubt Englishmen among them, who were now compelled to assist in providing food for the German army.

The *West Cumberland Times* reports on 26 August 1916 that there were German prisoners at Rowrah working at Kelton Head Stone quarry.

There is an article in the *Cumberland and Westmoreland Herald* of 26 January 1918 about Private John Weightman Kings Liverpool Regiment, being imprisoned from November 1917.

Just after the end of the war, on 30 November, an article appeared in the local press, covering the story of Private John Holmes, of the King's Liverpool Regiment. Private Holmes, of Wordsworth Street, Keswick was captured by the Germans on 28 March 1918. Being wounded in the leg and unable to walk, he was taken to the NCO PoW camp at Minden, which had a capacity of 18,000. After four months, he was transferred to Friedrichsfeld, considered to be a good camp, where he was made to work in the chemical factory close by. Here they were given a German mark a day and often worked for twenty-four hours, then a little rest and back to work. As they often had marks deducted for small offences, they seldom had any money to spend. Even if they had, Holmes said there

A section of the completed Friedrichsfeld POW camp.

was nothing in Germany they could buy. The women he saw were wearing paper dresses and paper boots with wooden soles. These boots cost from 80 to 150 marks a pair. English prisoners had their army boots taken from them and were given boots with wooden soles. They were fed

The main entrance to the Friedrichsfeld camp during normal daily activities.

on sauerkraut, mangolds, cabbage and occasionally a potato. Holmes said he never saw another Keswick lad from the time he was taken prisoner. However, he saw the grave of Brigham old boy Private William Butterworth, 1st/10th King's (Liverpool Regiment), who was born in Cockermouth and whose home was also in Wordsworth Street.

In camp, the men slept on straw and when ill had three blankets and when well just two. They were clothed by the British Red Cross. They were allowed to walk around the town and could tell the Armistice was coming from glimpses in the German papers.

With around 150 others, Holmes left Freidrichsfeld on Sunday 17 November 1918, walked to two-and-a-half miles to the station and after a five hour ride reached Zevenear in Holland where they had a great reception. The next day, they left for Rotterdam where they were re-clothed and on the Tuesday placed on the Portuguese ship Porio (previously the German SMS *Prinz Heinrich*) with 2,000 others, including civilians and officers. The voyage across lasted from Tuesday to Friday. When they arrived in Hull, they were sent to Ripon Camp where Holmes was given two months' leave. He was very cheerful after all he had been through, but he said he never wanted to see Germany again as long as he lived

According to the *West Cumberland Times* of 25 January 1919, German prisoners George Schon, Wilheim Munk and Friedrich Herche were sentenced at the Assizes to six months in prison for stealing, killing and eating a sheep while at the Wasdale Head billots, from Rowrah Camp. The defence included that they thought the sheep was in pain.

On 15 January 1915, Cumberland Council Education committee reported that 39 of its employees had joined HM Forces: two attendance officers, five headteachers, twenty-one certified assistant teachers, six uncertified teachers and five other staff. In April 1915, Mr J Reay, schoolmaster at

SMS *Prinz Heinrich*. She was scrapped in 1920.

Rosthwaite School, Borrowdale, had joined the army. On 22 April, it was reported that 'subject to the approval of the County Education Committee, the managers have appointed his wife, who is a certified teacher, to take his place during his absence'. Private Caleb Barnes, Lancashire Fusiliers, was a student teacher at the time of enlisting in May 1916 and later became the headteacher of Braithwaite primary school.

Barnes was a prisoner in World War One and, although some reports say he was in Italy, he was taken prisoner in Belgium so would have been in prison in Germany. He wrote poetry and an account of his time as a prisoner.The following is from the Mid-Cumberland and *North Westmorland Herald* 27 April 1918,

'Mr and Mrs Herbert Barnes, Braithwaite have received a postcard from their second son, Caleb Barnes, signaller in the Lancashire Fusiliers, stating that he is a prisoner of war in Germany. He is an old Keswick School boy and at the time of enlisting in May, 1916, was a student teacher at Braithwaite School. He is 20 years of age, and his elder brother, Thomas Dixon Barnes, went out to India with the first draft of Territorials in 1914.'

Caleb Barnes had a true sense of vocation and loved his job dearly.

He was still on the War Office missing list two months later. Barnes was born in Braithwaite and attended the local school where he won a scholarship to Keswick School. As his school days neared an end he volunteered for service in the army and joined the Lancashire Fusiliers as a private soldier with Service Number 306965, to fight in France and Belgium. He took part in the battles of Ypres and Cambrai, during which he was taken prisoner. On his return to civilian life he studied at York College where he trained to be a teacher. His brother Thomas Dixon Barnes, 8th Border, went out to India with the first draft of Territorials in 1914. He worked as a farm labourer in 1911.

The first Keswick man to return from a German prison camp was Lance-Corporal John Thomas Telford of Wordsworth Street, who was discharged on 24 July 1919. The *Penrith Herald* of 1 December 1917 and the *Lancashire Evening Post* of 1 December 1917 report that Lance-

Corporal Telford, of Tithebarn Street, Keswick, won the Military Medal for good work done in the advance on Polygon Wood in Belgium (26 September to 3 October 1917). He was trained in alpine plant work at Keswick, and was in the alpine gardens of Lord Battersea at Cromer when war broke out. The *Lancashire Evening Post* of 3 January 1919 reports the repatriation of Northumberland Fusilier Colonel Lee Lewthwaite of Keswick.and Mr Asquith of Radcliffe Place,who was a returned PoW.

LANCE-CORPORAL TELFORD, Leicestershire Regiment, whose parents live in Tithebarn-street, Keswick, has been awarded the Military Medal for good work done in the advance on Polygon Wood. He was trained in the growing of Alpine plants by Mr. T. R. Hayes, Keswick, and was was trained in the growing of Alpine plants belonging to Lord Battersea at Cromer, and later into a leading establishment at Loughborough.

John Telford. *(Penrith Herald).*

Not all prisoners of war lived to return home. Private Geoffrey Bateson, Machine Gun Corps Infantry, was reported missing on 10 April 1918, during the first days of the Battle of the Lys (7-29 April 1918), part of the 1918 German offensive in Flanders. Bateson, of Penrith Street, Keswick, died as a PoW in Germany on 24 November 1918 and is buried in the Commonwealth plot at Berlin South-Western Cemetery. He was the son of Joshua, a labourer, and Sarah Bateson of Catherine Cottages, Keswick.

Private William Butterworth, 1st/10th King's Liverpool Regiment, son of William and Margaret Butterworth of Wordsworth Street, Keswick, worked as a grocer before the war. He died as a PoW and was buried at Cologne Southern Cemetery. 'On a postcard sent home, he [Butterworth] says everybody is very good to us, and we have our wounds treated just like in Blighty.' the *Lancashire Evening Post* on 7 January 1918 reported.

Private Fred Kendall, 8th Border, of Greta Hamlet, Keswick, was the son of Edward and Sarah Kendall of Score Crag, Grasmere and husband of Alice Kendall. He worked as a gardener in Keswick prior to enlisting in September 1915. He was taken prisoner on 11 April 1918, during the battle of the Lys, a famously dark day for the British forces as they were pushed back by the Germans. For the next five months, he

Limburg POW camp (capacity 12,000). Limburg was mainly used for Irish POWs, part of a plan by Germany and Sir Roger Casement, a former British diplomat, to involve Irish nationalists in an 'Irish Brigade' against Britain.

was held at the PoW camp in Limburg in the region of Hessen, Germany where he died, apparently of starvation, on 4 September 1918, aged 31. He was buried at Terlincthun British Cemetery on the outskirts of Boulogne, France.

Showers in Limburg Camp.

Chapter 8

Employing German Prisoners of War

In May 1913, German-born Fritz Weber began work as 'second coffee room waiter' at the Keswick Hotel. By the end of the following year, he was one of thousands of German nationals held as prisoners on the Isle of Man. His English wife of five years, Minnie (nee Temple) was left to bring up their children, William, Elsie and Edith, on her own, and with no income to provide for them. In turn, Minnie was declared an 'alien'

Fritz Weber (front row, left) outside the Keswick Hotel with fellow employees in 1913. *(Cumberland and Westmorland Herald)*

and was required to report to the police as a German national, despite being born and bred in the UK. In July 1917, Fritz and Minnie's youngest daughter Edith died; she was just two years old. His release to see her on compassionate grounds was still being negotiated at the time and was cancelled following her death.

Minnie's designation as an 'alien' remained despite one of her brothers, Private Cyril Temple, 8th Border, being killed in action on 9 September 1917 and posthumously receiving the British War Medal and Victory Medal. Cyril Temple is commemorated at St Cuthbert's Church, West Walls, Carlisle – both on the parish memorial and on their Boys' Brigade memorial.

In July 1917, the *Carlisle Journal* carried a feature under the headline 'Employment of German PoWs'. This stated that the county highways committee had asked Arlecdon and Frizington councils to 'apply to the government for the use of PoWs in improving the approaches to Rowrah Bridge'. The Journal reported in March 1918 that '130 Germans were taken back to Rowrah after a day's work'. The *West Cumberland Times* reported on 30 January 1918 on German PoWs on the land, stating 6,000 have been employed on the land for some time past and that they worked in gangs of four of five under the supervision of an English soldier and policeman ploughman, the latter acting as gang foreman. They were not sent willy-nilly to farms – rather the farmers chose the ones they liked.

There was a prisoner of war camp which was variously called by the following four names: Lamplugh/Rowrah; Arlecdon; Salter; Hey Leys meadows. It was a satellite of Leigh in Lancashire, a POW camp located within a mill. The men in charge at Lamplugh were the South Wales Borderers.

The Lamplugh POW camp consisted of rows of wooden huts with associated gardens, and many of its POWs were engaged in farming or forestry

All the prisoners who died at the camp are now buried at the German War Cemetery at Cannock Chase, Staffordshire (Block 14), established in 1956. One, Vinscent Suchanak aged 29, was accidentally killed working in a quarry on 5 May 1917 and was initially buried in the churchyard of St Joseph's, Frizington. He had only worked in the quarry for a few days (the inquest report is in the *WN* 10 May 1917), had been transferred from Leigh on 7 November 1916 and originally came from Proboshowitz, Silesia, Germany. There were another ten who died as a result of influenza (November/December 1918): seven were first buried

The German Cemetery on Cannock Chase contains the bodies of all German servicemen who died in the UK during both world wars.

in the churchyard at St Michael's Church, Lamplugh (where the parsonage stood in the corner of the churchyard) and the others in St Joseph's, Frizington.

The determining factor for the place of burial at that time would have been their religion. One good thing about their re-interment at Cannock Chase is they were buried in adjacent graves regardless of whether they were Protestants or Catholics. The agreement about these graves being transferred to the new German War Graves Cemetery at Cannock Chase was made in 1959. It is believed that the Lamplugh/Frizington ones were transferred in 1961 but there is no exact date. The transfer of the grave of Fritz Reich from Whitehaven Cemetery would have been about the same time.

The seven German POWs who were initially buried at Lamplugh were as follows: Wilhelm Georg Fritz Wengel; Emil Richard Fritz Blanke; Heinrich Hellweg; Adolf Heuer; Karl Otto Pretzsch; Fritz Timm; and Adolf Gustav Schomann.

Chapter 9

Victoria Cross winners

Cumberland had more Victoria Cross (VC) recipients per capita of population during the First World War than anywhere else in England. Nine VCs were won in a county with a population of 265,746 (1911 census), 0.34 per 10,000 population. The VC is the highest military decoration awarded for valour 'in the face of the enemy'.

James Alexander Smith VC was born in Workington as James Alexander Glenn on 5 January 1881 and is thought to have taken his mother's maiden name so he could enlist at the age of 13 into the Third Militia Battalion. He served as a regular soldier and was discharged into the Army Reserve but was called up in August 1914 and sent overseas. Private Smith and his Border regiment colleague Private Abraham Acton of Whitehaven, eight miles south of Workington, were awarded their medals for conspicuous bravery on 21 December 1914 at Rouges Bancs near Armentieres, northern France. They voluntarily went from their trench to rescue a wounded man who had been lying against the enemy's trench for 75 hours. And on the same day, again leaving their trench voluntarily under heavy fire, they brought into cover another wounded man. They were under fire for an hour whilst conveying wounded men to safety.

In March 1915, three months after his courageous acts with Acton, Private Smith was wounded and returned to Workington. (A separate report says 16 April 1915). The *West Cumberland Times* recorded how Smith was given a hero's welcome as he arrived home by the last train from Carlisle:

> 'That he did not manage entirely to avoid the welcome waiting for him was due to his being "spotted" on the train at Wigton. The news was wired on to Maryport and from Maryport to Workington.'

He was hoisted shoulder high and carried through the streets. Workington mayor Alderman P Walls presented him with a medal and a purse containing twenty-five sovereigns. He served overseas until January 1917, returned to England and was finally discharged on 8 January 1919. His medals were bequeathed to the Border Regiment and are on display in the regimental museum at Carlisle Castle. He is named on the Regimental VC Memorial, Carlisle Cathedral.

Acton, who enlisted at Whitehaven in the 5th Border (TF) and then transferred to the 2nd Border in January 1914 as a regular solider, did not survive to receive his medal. He was killed in action at the Battle of Festubert, France on 16 May 1915, aged 22, and his body was never found. He is named on the Le Touret Memorial to the Missing. His VC was presented to his parents by King George V at Buckingham Palace on 29 November 1916. Acton, an Orangeman, is also named on the Ulster Tower memorial at the Thiepval Memorial to the Missing.

One of the most striking features of the Great War is the enormous amount of poetry it inspired. The news in February 1915 that the King had bestowed the VC to Acton and Smith inspired Hardwicke Rawnsley to write a poem (date unknown) in honour of these two soldiers. entitled December 21st.

December 21st

When at Red Banks, companions tried and true,
You ventured all to save a brother man,
When with your precious burdens back you ran
And showed what gallant Borderers dare and do,
More than your soldier-mates took note of you,
The very angels who with your longing scan
This earthly stage were glad; your saviour-plan
Thrilled Heaven's great armies watching from the blue.
Wherefore today all Cumbrian hearts rejoice
To think the Viking warrior in your blood
Has learned of Christ the noblest knightliest thing;
To know you fearless made it the hero's choice,
And for your country's honour and your king
Have proved the deathless might of brotherhood.

Chapter 10

The men who fought

Sergeant James William Downie, 8th Border, eldest son of Charles and Sarah Jane Downie (nee Graves) of Greta Villas, Keswick, a waller's apprentice for Timothy and a Brigham old boy, received the Military Medal for conspicuous bravery in general engagements. His parents received a letter from Captain JE Stuart, Signalling Section, 8th Border (printed in the Penrith Herald on 9 September 1916), to inform them of the medal. Stuart described Downie 'as his right hand in England, in the trenches, in training the men, and in action'. Downie had been removed from the battalion because he was wounded in action and he was in a Birmingham hospital, aged 24, with a compound fracture of the right arm.

Private Fred Brownrigg, 2nd/8th Lancashire Fusiliers, was an old pupil of Crosthwaite School. Previous to his enlisting, he was serving his apprenticeship with Mr J.B. Fleming, grocer, Market Square, and for some time he was errand boy for Mrs Frances of Station Street. He was so keen to serve his country that he enlisted before he reached army age, and was barely 19 years old when he met his death on the battlefield. As a stretcher bearer in the Lancashire Fusiliers, he saw much service immediately behind the firing line and had some very narrow escapes. Whilst rescuing wounded comrades on 27 July 1917, he received terrible injuries from an enemy shell and died two days later.

The Military Medal was awarded to Brigham old boy Corporal James Chapman, 2nd Border, the son of John and Grace of Leonard Street, Keswick and husband of Florence May Chapman of Southey Street. They married on 14 September 1917 at St John's Parish Church and had been married only five weeks when Chapman was killed in action on 26 October 1917. She was awarded a pension of 15 shillings a week from 24 June 1918. His parents were told in a letter that he went over the top in charge of a Lewis gun team and was soon after hit in the head and killed outright. He had been a shoemaker for Mr Ritson, Station Street, Keswick (whose son Joseph, Border, voluntarily listed in November 1914 though under military age, and died on 19 May 1917 aged 19) before enlisting on 4 December 1915. He went to France on 23 June 1916 and was recommended for the Military Medal on 3 October 1917. He is commemorated on the Tyne Cot Memorial, West-Vlaanderen,

The Lewis gun is a World War One-era light machine gun of American design that was perfected and widely used by the British Empire.

Belgium. It bears the names of almost 35,000 officers and men whose graves are unknown. Also on the Tyne Cot Memorial are Private David Cannon, 24th Manchester Regiment, son of Daniel and Margaret Cannon of Bassenthwaite, and Harrison Earl, 7th Border, only son of Robert Earl of Threlkeld. Cannon, who worked as a servant in 1901, enlisted in Keswick.

Gunner George Cowperthwaite Royal Field Artillery, son of John and Mary Cowperthwaite of High Briery, Keswick, worked as a wood turner at the Briery Bobbin Mill before the war and is buried at Quarry Cemetery, Montauban, Somme. A Brigham old boy, he was killed in action. Captain Nicholson, in a letter to his father printed in the *Penrith Herald* on 2 September 1916, said:

'It is with great regret that I write to inform you of the death of your son, Gunner George Cowperthwaite, who was killed yesterday morning (20 August 1916). I took him out with me at 4am yesterday, together with another signaller to make a survey of a new trench which had been dug during the night. We had finished the job and were just starting back when a trench mortar bomb fell right between us.

'It knocked all three of us to the ground and on recovering I regret to say your son was dead, he had been walking in the centre and the bomb must have exploded right at his feet. We buried him as best we could in a shell crater, but we were under heavy fire all the time. I have marked the spot and when the line advances a bit further – which I hope will be soon – I will have a proper mound made over the grave.

'Meanwhile I have had a cross up near the guns, it will be a consolation to you to know that he suffered no pain as he was killed instantly. He was a brave lad and always cheery and unconcerned when under fire, he will be a great loss to the Battery Please accept my sincerest sympathy and that the Officers and NCOs and men of the Battery in your great and sad loss.'

Cowperthwaite is mentioned on the family headstone in St John's churchyard.

Rifleman James Nelson Dover, 2nd Kings Royal Rifles, who died on 20 September 1914, was Keswick's first victim of the war. Brigham old boy Dover, of Banks Place, Keswick, left for the front on 12 September, and died of natural causes on a train from base at Havre to the firing line. The men who were with him attributed his death to exposure. Dover was buried at St Desir War Cemetery, France. He was a handy-man with Anthony Spedding of The Storms and he married a daughter of Mr E Wise, a shoemaker. He had two children.

James Nelson Dover.

Keswick is a perfect place for walkers wishing to cover the Scafells. On 20 April 1914, British climber Private Siegfried Herford, Royal Fusiliers, climbed Scafell's Central Buttress in two separate visits, but was killed in service by a grenade blast in the trenches of Flanders on 28 Feburary 1916 before he could return to climb it in one. Many others of the newly-formed Fell and Rock Climbing Club (FRCC) were killed in service; Corporal J Neville Fletcher was the first, dying

Gentlemen climbers: Siegfried Herford and George Mallory, an English mountaineer, on Pen-Y-Pass, north-west Wales 1912.

from wounds received at Ypres on 26 April 1915. The 1915 *Journal of the Fell and Rock Climbing Club of the English Lake District* was entitled *War Issue; Mountaineering Adventures at Home and in the Lands of Our Allies; Letters from the Front.*

There is a stained glass window to Herford at the Outward Bound, Eskdale, West Cumbria. He is buried in Brown's Road Military Cemetery, Festubert, France. He is also commemorated on the Great Gable War Memorial. He was the son of Charles H and Marie Catherine

Herford (nee Betge) of Parkfield Road, Didsbury, Manchester. His mother came from Bremen, Germany and it is believed that the marriage took place there as it cannot be traced in British records. His father Charles was Professor of English Literature at Manchester University and was at least second generation British. He belonged to the large Teutonic population of Manchester, many of whom were Unitarian, as were the Herford family. So why is there a window to him in Eskdale? Originally it was in a 'Chapel' in Manchester. Almost certainly this was Cross Street Chapel. This was, and is, the main Unitarian Church in central Manchester. The chapel was destroyed during a World War Two air raid in December 1940 and subsequently rebuilt. The window was transferred to the Outward Bound Centre at Eskdale in 1976.

At the unveiling of the plaque on 8 June 1924 by FRCC president Dr Arthur Wakefield, the tablet was draped in the Union Jack that had flown on HMS *Barham*, the flagship of the 5th Battle Squadron at the Battle of Jutland.

The old plaque was removed on 10 July 2013 by the Royal Engineers. A replacement plaque was installed in September 2013, also by the Royal Engineers, and unveiled on 10 November 2013 at a ceremony attended by John M Barrett, Club President. The old memorial was moved to the Armitt Museum. Ambleside. Originally one of the twenty names was a BH Witty. This was an error and his name was actually BH Whitley – the memorial was revised in September 2006. Whitley was killed in action on 9 July 1916. BH Witty died in 1922 from pneumonia. It was designed by WG Collingwood. The FRCC Journal 1922-24

Cross Street Chapel, c 1835.

includes a detailed map of the land that was part of the memorial scheme. It is at Armitt Library in Ambleside. In 1926, land was bought by the National Trust in the Ennerdale valley, as part of the memorial scheme, to provide accessibility to the higher reaches of Steeple, Pillar, Kirk Fell, Great Gable, Brandreth, Haystacks and Red Pike.

The FRCC bought Great Gable and 12 surrounding fells in 1923 as a permanent memorial for the club members who had sacrificed their lives in the First World War. The fell tops were then given to the National Trust.

Brigham old boy Corporal Thomas Allan Hodgson, 8th Border, youngest son of Timothy and Mary Ann Hodgson of Blencathra Street, Keswick, enlisted in September 1914 and was sent to France in September 1915. On the night of 20 January 1916, he was reported missing believed killed. The following was conveyed to Mr Hodgson in a letter written by Captain Wilfred Gardiner Cassels, 8th Border, a friend of Corporal Hodgson:

> 'Your son went out with the scout officer and two other men on a patrol last night at 9.30pm, and neither your son or the officer have been seen since. I was not in the line at the time, and heard about this sad case only at 1am, but I have done my best to try and find out what happened.
>
> 'Next morning we searched and searched the place from all sides with telescopes, but could see nothing except that a wire entanglement had been pulled to one side, as if to allow a party to pass through. We are hoping the Germans will put up a notice, as they have done on previous occasions to say whether these two were killed or what happened. May I offer you my heartfelt sympathies for this sad event. You may be sure that if anything more comes to light I will let you know at once. I will try to arrange his personal belongings to be taken over by some man going on leave as there will be less chance of getting lost.'

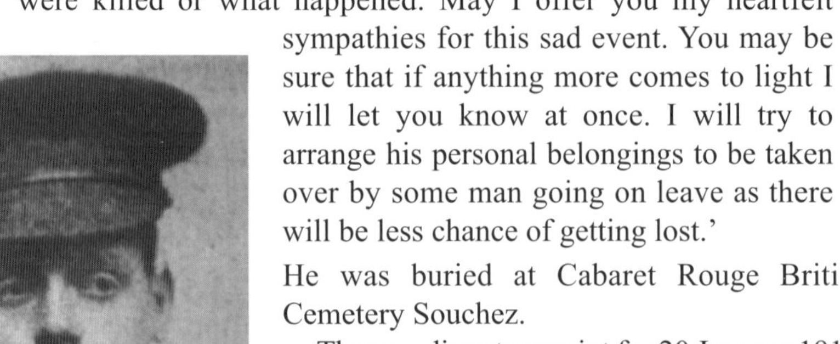

He was buried at Cabaret Rouge British Cemetery Souchez.

The war diary transcript for 20 January 1916, by Lieutenant-Colonel CE Bond, who took over command of the 8th Border, relates to a quiet day at Ploegsteert. He said that Colonel Winston Churchill, who had left government and enlisted in the army after the spectacular

Mark Mayson.

failure of the Gallipoli campaign, had inspected their lines with a view to taking them over during the night. Lieutenant Warren and Corporal Hodgson were on patrol. They did not return and no evidence was forthcoming as to what happened to them.

William and Mary Mayson of St Herbert's Street, Keswick had five sons. When war broke out, her son Sergeant Mark Mayson, 5th (Royal Irish) Lancers, was in Dublin and was not long in being boarded – with the rest of his colleagues – on transport, according to the *Penrith Observer* of 19 January 1915. It reported:

> 'With such mystery was the matter shrouded at first the men thought they were coming to England, and it was not for some time that they realised their destination was much nearer the seat of action. While approaching the French coast, they received a bit of a fright. A destroyer suddenly appeared out of the darkness and brought their ship to a quick standstill by firing an alarm shot, to be followed by the bright glare of a searchlight. The Germans are in to us, sang out some of the men, but their alarm was of very short duration, for after ascertaining the nature of the vessel, the patrolling watchdog - which proved to be French – slipped away into the blackness again. Arriving in France, Mayson entrained on to Thursday morning, and by the evening his regiment was in touch with the enemy at a village called Brae. Here a German aeroplane was in evidence, and the British – many of whom had never seen aircraft before – found the novelty quite pleasing. 'But,' said Mayson, 'they soon wished it had been far away.''

On 17 June 1915, Henry Marshall married Florence Forrester of Blencathra Street, Keswick at Crosthwaite Church. The bridegroom, an assistant master at Brigham School, had recently enlisted in the 4th Border Regiment and was married in uniform.

Brigham old boy William Henry Watt (Harry) was born at 22 Rose Cottage, Keswick, the son of John, the coal agent at Keswick Station, and Mary Watt. Harry Watt was living in Springsure, Queensland, Australia when he travelled to Rockhampton to enlist in late 1915. He joined the 25th Australian Infantry (AIF), arriving in Plymouth on 2 November 1916 and Etaples, France on 14 December, finally reaching his unit in the line on 20 February 1917. In his last letter home, dated 16 September 1917 'to my Dear Mother, Brothers and Sisters', he refers to the great battle he is going into: the assault along Westhoek Ridge facing Glencorse Wood on 20 September 1917.

'This is my last. I am going into something great soon, and I may never come out again. I am going in with a good will and I don't feel frightened to die. We will all meet again in heaven I hope. And this must be God's wish, don't fret or worry over me, but God's will be done. My message to James is to always be good and stick to his mother. I haven't time to write to you all. And I am only allowed the one letter now. We are well up to the front, and the guns are thundering something terrific. So mother dear look on the bright side of things. I know life's sweet but we have all got to die sometime. There are thousands besides me that may never come out, and their all some poor mother's sons. I hope that it will soon be over and that you will soon all be happy at home again. Write to Claire for me. I haven't left a letter for her … So now I will close with deepest love to you all. I trust you will all be comfortable and happy until God calls you all into his fold where parting shall be no more. Mrs Evans will give this to you.

'So God bless and keep you all safe in his keeping. I am quite prepared to die. So Good bye till we meet again in heaven I hope. Always your loving son Harry.

Harry Watt came through this battle in one piece, only to be killed in action in the attack on Broodsiende Ridge on 4 October 1917. The battle lasted from 4-7 October. He has no known grave, but his name is on the Menin Gate along with more than 54,000 other soldiers lost without known

22 Rose Terrace, Keswick.
(Cumbrian Cottages self-catering).

graves from the Battle of Ypres.Also commemorated on the Menin Gate is Private Edward Wood, Northumberland Fusiliers, born in Keswick.

Many people left England for Australia and Cumberland played its part. Private Robert Beatham, VC born in Glassonby near Penrith, also enlisted in the AIF. He was educated at a local school and as a teenager, he emigrated to Australia with his brother Walter. He was one of nine sons, and seven of the Beatham brothers served in the War, as did their father. Three of the brothers were to die in the conflict within five months of each other.

Fanny Evans lived next door to Harry Watt's mother at Number 21. Fanny lost her son, Edwin Evans, 8th Border, on 10 April 1918 at Ploegsteert, not far from where Harry had been killed. Evans, who was born in Portinscale, Keswick, also has no known grave but is commemorated on a local memorial.

Brigham old boy Private Fred Scott Martin, 8th Border, son of John Martin, of Heads House, Keswick, and Brigham old boy Private Robert Bertram 8th Border, of Rose Terrace, Keswick were killed on the same day as Evans. Bertram, whose father was manager of the Briery Bobbin Mill, first arrived in France on 29 September 1915 (the obituary in Keswick Reminder on 10 April 1918 states that he was previously reported missing). Martin, whose father was registrar for the Keswick district, was a partner with D.N. Paper, in a large estate agency. He was well-known in the Lake District as a rugby footballer, and he was a St Bees School old boy. The *Lancashire Evening Post* of 14 May 1918 reports:

> 'The death of Quartermaster Fred S Martin, Keswick, adds emphasis to the record of the old Rugby team associated with Keswick. Members of this team at the outbreak of war rallied to the country's call, and roused such enthusiasm that 60 lads joined the Border Regiment in one week. Seventy old players of the team are known to have joined the colours.'

Mr T.T Messenger, Keswick compiled for the *Lancashire Evening Post* in May 1918 the following list of a team who represented Keswick in one well-remembered match: Private Stainton Clark (killed); Private Chas Clark, Corporal Mark Davey (killed); Sergeant Louis Foster (killed); Sergeant Frank Gardiner (killed); Captain Chas Hodgson (killed); Lieutenant Harvey Hodgson (killed); Corporal Alan Hodgson (killed); Lieutenant AW Huckett (killed); Lieutenant HC Huckett (killed);

Horace Westmorland.

Lieutenant A Johns (killed); Quartermaster FS Martin (killed); Sergeant Tom Sanders (killed); Lieutenant Bert Sanderson (wounded); Sergeant Walter Swinburn (wounded); and Lieutenant Colin Warwick (killed).

Lieutenant Colonel Horace 'Rusty' Westmorland OBE flourished in the pre-war British climbing scene. In 1912, he was invited to take a commission in a Canadian Territorial Highland Regiment. He qualified at Military School and was transferred to the Canadian Regular Army where he served in Belgium and France from 1915 to 1919.

Maymyo was the home in Keswick of John Tomlinson Wilson known to all as Tom Wilson 'T PUP Chap', according to Keswick Characters by the Keswick Historical Society and the Friends of Keswick Museum & Art Gallery. He became well-known for his charity work and his articles in the Keswick Reminder in Cumbrian dialect.

His service life began at the age of 27 with mobilisation of the 4th Battalion of the Border Regiment (TF) in August 1914. He and his companions, recruited from Carlisle and district, east Cumberland, Brampton, Penrith, Keswick and the whole of Westmorland, travelled to Carlisle then on to Walney Island at Barrow. They were joined by men from Kendal. It was presumed that there would be some further training taking place which the men would continue in Sittingbourne, Kent, where the battalion arrived in September. Towards the end of September, Lord Kitchener decided to send three divisions of Territorials to India to replace the regular troops which were needed to fight as usual. There was a promise that at the end of six months, they would return. The Territorials were told that they 'would have all the honours of the war just as if they had gone to France'.At the end of October, the Territorials sailed from Southampton for Bombay in HMS *Deseado* (launched by Harland & Wolff, Belfast in October 1911 for Royal Mail Steam Packet services to West Indies and South America) and arrived in Rangoon early in December to relieve the 1st Borders.

One of the officers was Lieutenant Percy Mirehouse Hope from Keswick, an architect, whom Wilson knew quite well. The Battalion arrived in Maymyo and moved to their quarters, which had until recently been occupied by the 1st Borders, a regular battalion that had just returned to England. Somewhere in India, the two trains carrying the 4th and 1st Battalions passed each other, the 4th heading east and the 1st heading west. Soon members of the Battalion were sent to Mandalay where the tribes who lived in the Kachir Hills had become 'troublesome' and perhaps Wilson, with members of the Battalion, were members of

Hope Park. Before 1925, the land was an area for the grazing of horses which were used to transport charabancs from Keswick Railway Station to the hotels in the town.

the 'small punitive expeditionary force' sent to move about the troubled area. That would have been Wilson's first experience of war action. But there were reminders of home in Burma. He remembered finding railway lines marked 'the Workington Iron & Steel Company'. Wilson was eventually promoted to Brigade Signals Sergeant and perhaps included in his duties was the supervision of those Turkish prisoners building the Botanical Gardens which still survive in Maymyo.

The Battalion remained in Burma until early 1918 when it was relieved and transferred to Jubbulpore in India. The war had ended and the Battalion left Peshawar in November 1919 to sail to Plymouth. The Territorials travelled by train first to Kendal and then to Carlisle, where they were demobilised on 31 January 1920.

Wilson and other Keswick men came home. He resumed working for the family business next to the Post Office and Lieutenant Hope, now Colonel Hope, returned to his architectural firm in Station Street.

Not all losses were among the fighting men. William Edgar Mounsey and his wife Fanny Sewell were both born in Keswick. When their eldest child, John Thomas was about four years old, they emigrated to the United States. They settled in Chicago and opened a business called Mounsey Movers. In 1914, Fanny had the opportunity to visit her family in Keswick. She and her travelling companions, Mrs John Fisher and Mrs

Fanny Mounsey - In Keswick, she worked as a servant and William as a general labourer.

Fisher's son Wilfred boarded the Canadian Pacific liner *Empress of Ireland* bound for Liverpool. On 29 May 1914, the *Empress of Ireland* was in a collision with the Norwegian collier *Storstad* and the Empress went down (of the 1,477 people on board, 1,012 died). Both ladies were lost and neither body was recovered. Almost a year later, the Mounsey family received word from England that a woman in a Liverpool institution named 'Kate Fitzgerald' was uttering the name 'Mounsey' and had a fear of water. She was believed to be a survivor of the *Empress of Ireland* disaster. William, his daughter Sarah Lund, born in Blufton, Indiana, and her husband Charles Lund travelled to New York to take the passenger ship *Lusitania* to Liverpool. The *Lusitania* was torpedoed and sunk by German U-boat *U-20* on 7 May 1915 off the south-west coast of Ireland (of the 1,962 passengers and crew aboard, 1,191 lost their lives). The ship's sinking helped shift public opinion in the US against Germany. William Mounsey's body was never recovered. Charles Lund's body was found and his remains returned home. Sarah Lund survived, spent time in hospital in Ireland and went to Liverpool to meet the woman in question, who proved not to be Fanny Sewell Mounsey, and returned to Chicago. The partially-collapsed wreck lies 11 miles off the Old Head of Kinsdale Lighthouse in 300ft of water.

The Reverend Francis H Bettison, curate of Crosthwaite and son of the Reverend Henry Albert Bettison and Mary Elizabeth Bettison (Lane) of Whitfield, Northumberland, was married to Dora Hadfield Edmondson daughter of the late Edward Edmondson of Knowle, Warwickshire, and Mrs Edmondson of Derwent Bank, Keswick at an earlier date than was originally intended because the bridegroom had received an order, having been commissioned in January 1914, to hold himself in readiness for dispatch to his duty as a Territorial Officer (1/4th Border). In the circumstances, only a few guests in the locality could be notified to attend. Four bridesmaids were to have been present, but only one was able to be there. Cyril Fox acted as best man. The Reverend Rawnsley performed the ceremony and in a short address referred to the unusual circumstances attending the marriage.

Mark Hedley Bettison worked at Lloyds Bank at Newburn on Tyne, Northumberland.
(Ryton and District War Memorials Project)

Francis Bettison was born in 1881 at Otterburn, Northumberland, where his father was then curate. Bettison was educated at Otterburn School, Barnard Castle public school and University College, Durham and was ordained in 1905 at Newcastle and was curate of Ponteland, Newcastle 1905-1909 and then curate of St John's Windermere from 1909-1910 and finally curate of Crosthwaite up to 14 August 1914. Crockfords, the authoritative directory of the Anglian Communion in the UK, states he technically remained curate until 1917. It is unusual to have been nine years as a stipendiary curate, as opposed to a perpetual curate.

We know that Bettison lost a brother, Mark Hedley Bettison, in the war, on 29 April 1916, at the age of 29.

From various issues of the *London Gazette*, we know that Francis Bettison had been a Territorial soldier in the Cumberland and Westmorland Yeomanry as early as 1912 when he was a 2nd Lieutenant. He was then commissioned into the 1st/4th Border Regiment Territorials in January 1914 and mobilised on 4 August 1914 (six days before his rushed marriage). He was sent to Burma in October 1914 where he served as a combatant for two years. In January 1914 he cites his address as 26, Stanger Street, Keswick (which is where he was lodging with the Younghusband family as a curate) Unfortunately his service documents seem to be in the 'burnt documents' (ie, lost in the Blitz in World War Two) but the *Whitehaven News* and the *London Gazette* help to piece together the story. His personal papers as chaplain survive in the

National Archives at Kew. On or about 10 November 1914, he was promoted to Lieutenant (*Whitehaven News* 12 November 1914), although he may have been demoted at some stage as the promotion occurs again in April 1916 (*Whitehaven News* 13 April 1916) shortly before the loss of his brother.

According to the *London Gazette* and the Ryton project (dedicated to the memory of those men and women from the former Ryton Urban District Council area who lost their lives whilst serving in the armed forces, or were killed by enemy action), he relinquished his commission in the Border Regiment (when he was apparently a 2nd Lieutenant again) on 22 October 1916 to become a Forces chaplain, although it is not reported locally until March 1917 in the *Whitehaven News*. As a chaplain, he served under the Archbishop of Bombay for 15 months in the Mesopotamia Base Hospital, Bombay until 20 January 1918. He was then released by the Government of India on account of urgent matters at home (details unknown) From shipping records, he can be traced arriving back in England from Bombay on 27 February 1918 (on the P&O ship *Nagoya*) so he had departed almost immediately. It seems possible that this course of events was influenced by the loss of his brother, although when his gratuity was being considered in 1920 it is stated that his appointment as chaplain was at the request of the Government of India – which does not preclude that he had approached the Indian Government in the first instance.He again became a 4th class temporary chaplain in July 1918 (*London Gazette*).

A letter sent on 19 July 1918 from Chaplain Dept, War Office: reads

> 'I am directed to inform you that you have been selected for duty as temporary chaplain to the Forces, 4th Class, and should report yourself to the Officer Commanding, Codford, Wilts, on the 1st Aug next for duty at that station, notifying to this office the date on which you join. A voucher entitling you to a half-price rail ticket in respect of your journey is enclosed; please acknowledge receipt. Details as to conditions of service, etc are shown in the pamphlet "Notes on Service in the Army Chaplains' Department".'

A similar letter dated 19 July 1918 from same department was signed by EH Thorold, CF Staff Officer:

> 'I am directed to acquaint you that the Reverend Francis Henry Bettison has been appointed for duty as a Church of England temporary Chaplain to the Forces, 4th class at Codford, Wilts, and has ordered to report himself to the officer commanding at that station, on the 1st August next [which he did, at 11am] (Vice the

BE/1125 3/4

Temporary Chaplains engaged for duty abroad.

TO HIS MAJESTY'S PRINCIPAL SECRETARY OF STATE FOR THE WAR DEPARTMENT.

I, (name) Francis Henry Bettison.

of (address) Derwent Lodge Keswick Cumb^d

being a duly ordained {priest / minister} of the Church of England

hereby offer, and agree if accepted by you, to serve at home or abroad as a temporary Chaplain to His Majesty's Forces, 4th Class, with the relative rank of Captain in the Army while so employed, on the following conditions:—

1. The period of my service hereunder shall commence as from the day on which I shall commence duty abroad, and shall continue until the expiration of 12 calendar months thereafter, or until my services are no longer required, whichever shall first happen.

2. My pay and allowances shall (subject as hereinafter appears) be at the rate authorized for 4th Class Chaplains to the Forces. (The pay is 10s. 6d. a day, and the allowances vary according to circumstances.)

3. In addition to such pay, I shall receive a free passage to any country abroad to which I may be sent, and (subject as hereinafter appears) a similar free passage back to England.

4. I shall receive free rations while in the field and when considered necessary for the performance of my duties the use of a Government horse and forage.

5. During the said period I will devote my whole time and energies to my service hereunder, and will obey all orders given to me by superior Military or Naval Officers.

6. Upon the completion of each period of 12 months' continuous service as a commissioned chaplain (whether this be on or before the date of expiry of this contract), provided I shall have consistently performed my duties to your satisfaction in all respects, I shall receive a gratuity of 60 days' full pay at the rate hereinbefore specified. But in case I shall in any manner misconduct myself, or shall be (otherwise than through illness or unavoidable accident) unfit in any respect for service hereunder, of which misconduct or unfitness you or your authorised representative shall be sole judge, you shall be at liberty from and immediately after such misconduct or unfitness to discharge me from further service hereunder, and thereupon all pay and allowances shall cease, and I shall not be entitled to any free passage home or gratuity.

Dated this 28th day of October 1918

F. H. Bettison (Here sign.)

Witness to the signature of the said F. H. Bettison.

David F. McCreary. (Witness).

On behalf of the Secretary of State I accept the foregoing offer,

Francis Bettison's offer to serve as a temporary chaplain, dated 28 October 1918. *(Kew Archives)*

> Rev WH Gunter CF). While so employed he will be entitled to the pay at the rate of 10s 6d a day (which will be issued to him by the Army Agents, Sir CR McGrigor, BT and Co), and also, during the period of war, to (i) a free issue of rations (or allowance in lieu), and (ii) to field allowance if under canvas, and otherwise to lodging and fuel and light allowances, unless accommodated in public quarters or billets'.

He was on a 12 month contract.

On 3 July 1918, there is a fitness report - Age (last birthday) 37, height, ins - 71½ . Weight lbs 154. Hearing good. Teeth good. General health good. Fit. Remarks fit for general service at home and abroad. He was finally sent to France according to the following letter days before the end of the war.

> 'Letter from Chaplain's Dept, War Office, Piccadilly dated 18/10/1918 from EH Pearce. To say that Bettison has been selected for duty as temporary chaplain to the forces of the Expeditionary Force in France.
>
> 'You should report yourself to me, at the above address, on the 28th instant, between the hours of 10 and 12.30, ready to embark. Your address for letters will be c/o The Assistant Chaplain General, Boulogne, BEF France.'

At this date his address is given as Derwent Lodge, Keswick, the home of his wife's mother. He was in France until March 1919 and was granted a gratuity on leaving. Also from the *London Gazette* we know he was appointed as an honorary Forces chaplain on 27 October 1919. He was posted from the 5th Army to 52 Brigade on 11 November 1918 and on 6 March 1919 was granted leave to the UK presumably in connection with the birth of his second child. He was demobilised on 26 March 1919.

There is also a 'Protection Certificate' dated 7 April 1919 which seems to be the beginning of the process of awarding a gratuity/pension, although that issue dragged on well into 1920 and there is no clear evidence how it was concluded. But in April 1920, he was again living at Derwent Lodge, Keswick, as was Dora by the time of Audrey's baptism in 1915.

Quite rightly, a lot of attention has been given to those who lost their lives in the war but many who came back were not the same. Reginald Reeves served in the war along with his brothers, William Gill Reeves an engineer apprentice and Joseph Henry Reeves an engineer apprentice who all returned home. The Reeves family was originally from Mill Street, Maryport but Reginald Reeves settled in Keswick on his return.

He was plagued by ill health as he aged, having been gassed at the Battle of the Somme and taken prisoner.

Cecil Walker Birkbeck, 5th Border, son of Sarah Birkbeck of Stanger House, Keswick, and the late Thomas Henry Birkbeck, was a draper's assistant living at 40 Main Street, Keswick on enlistment on 24 September 1915. He contracted tuberculosis in April 1916 and was discharged as no longer fit for military service on 3 June 1916 with sixty percent war disability pension. He never recovered and died on 21 July 1919 aged 22. He is buried at St Kentigern, Crosthwaite

The *Lancashire Evening Post* of 6 September 1919 reports on the inquest held at Keswick concerning the death of Richard Wallace , who resided at Bridge Terrace, Keswick and was found lying dead in a field near Crosthwaite vicarage, with a bottle lying beside him which had contained a poisonous weed. The deceased was aged 34, and was a gardener for the Rev W.E Bradley, vicar of Crosthwaite, with whom he went to Keswick from Ulverston some time before when Mr Bradley succeeded Hardwicke Rawnsley as vicar of Crosthwaite. His widow stated that he was demobilised the previous March after service in the Army in Egypt and Palestine (some Divisions moved to Egypt as a base for operations at Gallipoli). His health suffered while he was abroad and he was troubled with insomnia and pains in his head. He said he could not settle down to his work again. Mr Atter, who held the inquest, returned a verdict of 'Suicide while of unsound mind', remarking that although the deceased did not lose his life in the war, it was through the war he had taken his life. The only Keswick memorial he is listed on is that of Crosthwaite Church (St Kentigern) where the vicar obviously showed compassion. He is buried at St Kentigern.

Thomas and Helen Brunton of Main Street, Keswick received word that their third son Private Tom Brunton, Border, was again wounded, this time very severely, and would be permanently disabled, reported the Penrith Herald of 1 December 1917. He was lying in the Canadian General Hospital at Etaples, France. Formerly, he worked as a grocer's clerk and enlisted as soon as he was 18.

One of the more eccentric characters who lived in the Forge area in Keswick, above the Greta, was Robert Wildman, or Willie as he was known, according to *The Greta* by Keith Richardson (2012). Wildman lost a leg – apparently in the First World War – and wore a wooden leg as a replacement. General Wilfrid Spedding, Keswick Councillor and ex-High Sheriff, bumped into Wildman on the street in Keswick one day and enquired as to his well-being, and Wildman told him that he was to all intents and purposes homeless. As a result, Spedding provided land for Wildman to build a small wooden bungalow near the rock tunnel and beside the millrace at the head of the Forge. A little wooden bridge over the millrace gave access to the property and its garden. Wildman lived alone in the bungalow for many years. The empty building is still there to this day.

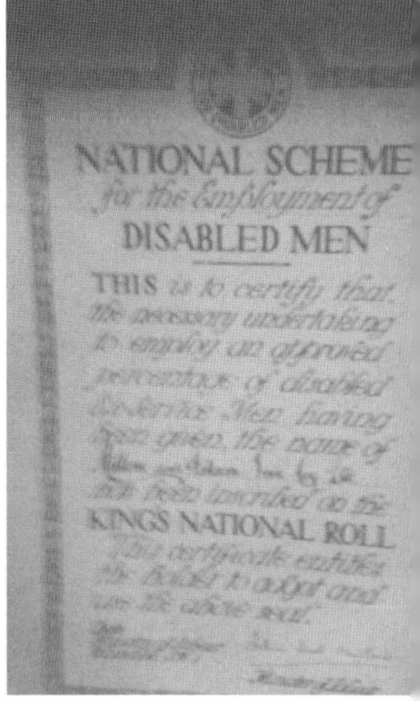

National Scheme for the Employment of Disabled Men: The disabled servicemen like their civilian colleagues wanted proper employment. Were ex-servicemen putting other disabled workers out of jobs?

Under the King's National Roll Scheme for the Employment of Disabled Men (certificate from scheme to the Millom and Askam Iron Co pictured below) that was started in 1919, Millom and Askam Iron Co, like other businesses, was obliged to employ an approved percentage of disabled ex-servicemen.

The *Sunderland Daily Echo* and *Shipping Gazette* of 6 October 1914 reported an inquest held in Keswick the previous day on John Thompson, a farm bailiff, who was found hanging at his home. It was stated that he had no domestic or business troubles. His daughter, in reply to the coroner, who asked if she could suggest any reason for her father being depressed, replied that she could not, unless it was that he read too much about the war. He was very fond of reading about the war and did so every day. He had no relatives at the front. The jury returned a verdict of 'Suicide whilst temporarily insane'.

In his monthly report, the Medical Officer for Health for Workington reported that the infant mortality in the first quarter of 1915 was one of the worst the town had ever had, 'viz two hundred per thousand births'. The Medical Officer said the main cases were the worst weather within living memory, and mental depression caused by the departure of so many men.

> 'One hears much in these days of women giving way to alcoholic excess in the absence of their husbands at the war. I am able to say emphatically that cases of this kind can scarcely be found in Workington. I know of only one case.'

Those away from home tried to keep in touch and those who couldn't fight themselves tried to support the troops as best they could. Hardwicke Rawnsley sent the following poem to the *Manchester Evening News* from Keswick. It relates to the planting of trees in

Manchester as tributes to soldiers (two teachers and 83 old boys at Blackley school) and was published in the newspaper on 18 March 1915:

Children, when you plant your tree
As a sure memorial,
One for each of eighty-three
Who obey'd their country's call.
Ask with more than common care,
All the neighbourhood give heed,
Pray to God that sun and air
Shower their blessing on your deed.
For these trees when we are shed
From the tree of mortal life,
Still shall speak of gallant deed,
Still record their bitter strife.
Still shall speak to far-off days
Of the school that gave its best,
And with gentle voice shall praise
Peace for peace not war is blest.

On 27 July 1915, he had filled a volume with his verse for the times, which he called *The European War 1914-15* (Century Press). There are marching songs and ballads, heroic episodes turned into ringing rhymes, a large number of commemorative sonnets and some reflective pieces. The collection closes with *At Wordsworth's Grave*: 'Wordsworth! An empire needs you at this hour. For now a second tyrant stands confest.'

In 1917, he retired from his post as vicar of Crosthwaite parish and spent his final years at Allan Bank, Grasmere, Wordsworth's old home. Close to Grasmere's war memorial is the 'Peace oak' planted by Rawnsley. He died in 1920 and was buried in the churchyard of his former parish at Crosthwaite. He left Allan Bank to the National Trust.

During the First World War, letter writing was the main form of communication between soldiers and their loved ones. The British Army Postal service delivered around 2 billion letters during the war. In 1917 alone, more than 19,000 mailbags crossed the English Channel each day, transporting letters and parcels to British troops on the Western Front. Censorship dictated what servicemen were permitted to disclose in their letters. However, in practice, men often found ways to impart information, and their letters offer a powerful and highly personal insight into the experience of war.

Private correspondence was censored. Military censors examined 300,000 private telegrams in 1916 alone. *(Imperial War Museum)*

In a letter home to his father Richard Fearon-Brown in Cockermouth, written on 15 August 1915, Sergeant Howard Irison Fearon Brown Royal Army Medical Corps, said:

> 'We have been in the thick of it, especially Sunday evening [15th August] when I was with the Dublin Fusiliers in their charge. It was an exciting time I can tell you! I was in the firing line in the afternoon and evening with the Dublin and Munsters. The firing was very heavy, the enemy simply rained bullets on us and men were shot on every side. The protection was very small – on some places only eighteen inches (two sandbags) high – so it was a rather difficult work dressing wounds when lying flat on the ground.'

He is remembered at the Doiran Memorial, Greece.

Chapter 11

War memorials, Keswick

Civic memorials to those lost in the First World War are usually straightforward to locate, as they were generally erected in prominent places. Additional memorials are also located in churches, and yet more in buildings that may not be readily accessible to the public. There are also war memorials that have now fallen into disuse and have been stored away, so that as a result they are no longer visible; these require the most persistence to locate. Not everyone who lost a relative in the First World War wanted their relative's name to appear on a memorial. One mother described in a letter, now preserved in Lancashire Record Office, that she felt this would merely act as a reminder of her loss every time she passed it.

The *West Cumberland Times* reported, on 10 April 1922, on a meeting of the Keswick Branch of the League of Nations Union where there was concern about the glorification of war. The realisation of the common sacrifice made by those from all backgrounds who served in the First World War and the corresponding need for equality of commemoration, was one of the guiding principles of Major General Sir Fabian Ware, the de facto founder of the Imperial War Graves Commission, now the Commonwealth War Graves Commission. With very few exceptions (less than thirty, the most celebrated being the Unknown Soldier buried in Westminster Abbey), repatriation of the dead from battlefields abroad was prohibited, irrespective of how illustrious the victim (this prohibition even included a grandson of Queen Victoria). They were also to be given the same memorials, with a general receiving an identical headstone to a private soldier. Furthermore, there were to be no class divisions when it came to burial, with officers buried alongside their men. The only notable exception occurred at the base hospital of Etaples, where officers were buried in a separate plot during the war and the arrangement was left unchanged when the formal cemetery was constructed.

Private Mark Lawrence Davey, 4th South African Infantry, son of John Thomas and Elizabeth Davey (Robson) of Keswick is buried at Etaples. He was a member of the Keswick volunteer fire brigade before

Keswick Cenotaph.

leaving for South Africa six years before the war. He was wounded in both legs by a shell at Delville Wood on 18 July 1916. His right leg was later amputated but he died of gangrene at the Canadian Hospital, Etaples. On 18 July 1916, the Germans made strong counter-attacks at Longueval and Deville Wood; they retook part of the latter.

The Keswick War Memorial, unveiled by Lord Rochdale and Walter Swinburn on 21 May 1922, is situated on the corner of Penrith Road and Station Street. It is a granite cenotaph-type memorial with slate plates and is dedicated 'To Keep Fresh the Memory of Our Brave Men who Fell in the Great Wars'. All the money for the memorial was raised by public subscription. The appeal for the original estimated £4,000 cost was launched in June 1919. In the first week alone, £950 was raised.

Joseph Banks Wivell, chairman of Keswick Council, insisted that the Fitz Park memorial land should be opened out, a high wall behind the Keswick Cenotaph taken down, and made the main entrance to the park, contending that this was the natural and best entrance (*Yorkshire Post* and *Leeds Intelligencer*, 21 April 1924). Why, therefore did the Keswick Cenotaph remain on its own island adjacent to but separate from Fitz Park? Between late 1923 and May 1924, the Royal British Legion and the War Memorial Committee, a local committee of townsfolk, led a group that held long and very heated meetings about Wivell's plans. They ultimately frustrated his plans. What it ultimately came down to was their belief that people who were just passing through the war memorial land as a thoroughfare, rather than to visit the Cenotaph, would desecrate the memorial and the land. Therefore, the Cenotaph only became available to those who were specifically visiting it. While not on private property and not hidden away, it is arguably not the focal point that Wivell intended

There was also an oak (or chestnut) tree planted in Upper Fitz Park – supplied by Kew Gardens,

Viscount Ullswater, Speaker of the House of Commons from 1905 to 1921 and MP for Westmorland for 25 years, married Mary Beresford-Hope

west London and grown from seeds from an oak tree at Verdun. It was planted on 24 September 1921 by James Lowther, 1st Viscount Ullswater.

This tree has not existed for many years now. It is not entirely clear where in the park it was planted, but most probably in the area directly behind the cenotaph. The *West Cumberland Times* of 17 August 1921 refers to the tree as an oak and the *Keswick Reminder* of 16 September 1921 refers to it as a chestnut. The figure of Victory, crowning a sheathed sword with a laurel wreath in memory of the dead, was carved in high relief. This was the work of Keswick-born artist Derwent Wood. When he was too old to enlist in the army at the onset of the First World War, he volunteered in the hospital wards and his exposure to the injuries inflicted by the new war's weapons led him to open a special clinic, the Masks for Facial Development Disfigurement Department (1917-1919) located in the Third London General Hospital, Wandsworth, south-west London. Each mask required many weeks of work. He constructed masks of thin metal, sculpted to

A 1906 portrait of Francis Derwent Wood by George Washington Lambert.

Memorial plaque to the fallen men of the CK&PR. *(Author)*

match the portraits of the men in their pre-war normality.

There is one panel, made from Skiddaw slate, commemorating the 109 names of the dead of the First World War. The 109 were solely from Keswick, as each of the surrounding villages had their own memorial to the fallen of that date. The names include: seven men with the surname Hodgson (Brigham old boys John H, John C, Isacc H, Allan, William, Frank, Joseph, and James); two Blamires, three Bousteads (Taylor, Laurence and William); two Dents (Brigham old boys Walter and Thomas); two Graves (Thomas and H); three Johns; two Riggs (Derwent Telford and Ernest); three Scotts; two Sewells; two Swinburns (Brigham old boys Joseph and John); two Swindles (Brigham old boys Peter William and Vipond Vickers); and two Towers (James and Maurice). There is one panel for men employed by the CK & PR who lost their lives in the First World War (seven names). This used to be in Keswick Railway Station until it was closed in 1972 and then moved to this location.

Grave of William Wallace Boustead at St John's Churchyard, Keswick. He returned from war but died in 1918.

The top ten surnames from the 1881 census in Keswick were (in order of incidence) Hodgson, Wilson, Scott, Atkinson, Smith, Robinson, Tyson, Walker, Harrison, and Swindle. The following are details of some of the men on the Keswick Cenotaph: Keswick road mender and poet Christopher Murray Boustead – whose works included *A Keswick Roadman* (1909) and a volume of poems entitled *A Few Rustic Lines* (1902) – and Annie Boustead who lost three sons to the war (Brigham old boys). Private Laurence Boustead, 7th Border, was killed in action (France and Flanders) on 23 April 1917 and is commemorated on the Arras Memorial. Private Taylor Boustead, 7th Border, was killed in action on the same day and is also commemorated on the Arras Memorial. Private Wallace William Boustead, 10th Border, signed up with his brothers but returned from the war with tuberculosis in 1917 and died a year later. He is buried at St John's Churchyard, Keswick. Their deaths were the end of the Boustead family in Keswick.

Brigham old boy Lance-Corporal Ernest Harford Dalzell, 1st Border, was the husband of Sarah Jane of Main Street, Keswick. He was the famous Cumberland and Westmorland fell runner who for six or seven years came first in the Grasmere sports. He also won fell climbs at Keswick, Eskdale, Ambleside, Ullswater and Bowness. He enlisted in June 1916. Prior to that, he kept a restaurant and ice cream shop facing Stanger Street, Keswick. He was hit in the neck by shrapnel after going over the top to take a German stronghold and died on 19 May 1917.

Walter and Thomas William Dent were sons of James and Elizabeth Dent of Station Road, Keswick. Lance-Corporal Walter originally enlisted in 1901 at Carlisle Castle. He later went on the Reserve and was recalled to the colours in August 1914 at which time he was a postman at Windermere, desiring some open-air occupation. The Battalion landed in Zeebrugge on 6 October 1914. They moved down to billets in Sailly sur Lys, north France, and were entrenched near Cordonnerie Farm, France where he was killed on 25 January 1915. He left a wife and six children under the age of nine at Stanley Terrace, Birch Street, Windermere.

His brother, Thomas, 2/4 Loyal North Lancs, enlisted at Colne, Lancashire on 2 February 1916. He went into the trenches for the first time on 14 February 1917 at Sailly Sur Leys and died on 10 March aged 39. He is buried at Pont du Hem Military Cemetery, La Gourge, west of Sailly. He left a wife, Mary Sarah, of Colne, Lancashire, and five children.

Sergeant Frank Gardiner, 8th Border, of Keswick died of wounds in France. After leaving Keswick School, he spent time in his father's carpenter's shop and also continued his studies, passing exams under the Board of Education in practical mathematics, solid geometry building construction and joinery. At the outbreak of war, he was a woodwork teacher at the Workington Secondary School, and for several years captained the Keswick Rugby football team. He went with the Border Regiment to Burma soon after the outbreak of war. On the expiration of his time of enlistment, he sought more active service. He returned to England, joined another battalion of the same regiment and was eventually drafted to France with his old rank of sergeant. He was seriously wounded on Sunday 22 October 1916 and conveyed to the base hospital. A leg was amputated on Friday 27, but later the same evening he passed away. He was the only remaining son of John and Mary Ann Gardiner of 93 Main Street, Keswick. He had four sisters and

George Mounsey is one of six recorded as lost on Roxburgh.

is buried at Wimereux Communal Cemetery, Pas de Calais, France.

Driver Tom Hetherington, Royal Field Artillery, lived on Herbert Street, Keswick, with his wife and one child. He worked as a butcher with Mr Adamson, Keswick before enlisting in September 1916. He was killed by a shell while visiting a Keswick friend in the same battalion on 27 May 1918 and is remembered on the Soissons Memorial, Aisne, France.

Thomas, Stephen and Arthur Johns were sons of Mr and Mrs B Johns of Eskin Place, Keswick. Private Thomas Johns, 25th Battalion Royal Fusiliers, died of dysentery in German East Africa. Brigham old boy Second-Lieutenant Stephen Johns, Royal Engineers, was killed by a shell on 14 March 1916. He was at his post of duty and another man was killed by the same shell during a slight gas attack. He was buried two miles behind the firing line in a little cemetery of apple trees. Second-lieutenant Arthur Johns, Royal Engineers, was killed in action on 25 September 1917 while about 100 yards back from the front line. Some of his men were wounded by a shell and he was helping to put one of the wounded on a stretcher when another shell killed him instantly. He was educated at Kendal Grammar School, and later at Keswick High School under the Reverend Cecil Grant When his school days were over, he underwent a course of training for engineering under the Camborne School of Mines, Cornwall. He held important posts as an engineer in Nigeria and returned to England just before the outbreak of hostilities.

Brigham old boy George Alwyn Mounsey, 3rd Engineer, SS Roxburgh, the third son of Mr and Mrs G Mounsey of Blencathra Street, Keswick, was lost after British steamer SS *Roxburgh* was sunk by the

German submarine *UC-74* 15 miles of Cape St John, Crete on 5 March 1918. Six of her crew were lost. Mounsey was last seen in the engine room. *UC-74* was credited with sinking thirty-seven ships, either by torpedo or by mines laid. The First World War section of the Tower Hill Memorial, London commemorates almost 12,000 Mercantile Marine casualties who have no grave but the sea. Mounsey's name can be found under the name of Roxburgh Newcastle.

Private Ernest Rigg, 7th Border, and Brigham old boy Private Derwent Telford Rigg, sons of John and Jane of Main Street, Keswick, were killed in the 2nd battle of Arras on 23 April 1917. Ernest Rigg worked as a postman on the Thornthwaite round.

Edmund Leck Sanders, 1st Border, of The Headlands, Keswick, was born in Dalton-in-Furness and married Mary Margaret Robinson in Keswick in 1904. Commemorated on the Helles Memorial, he was killed in action in Gallipoli on 21 August 1915. He was listed as missing in action and it was not until 1916 when one of his friends came forward to say he had died in action that the family received a pension; there were six children to bring up. Edmund's older brother Thomas William Sanders went to Canada where he died in a coal mine on 26 December 1919, in Nanaimo on Vancouver Island, BC.

Brigham old boy James Scott 2nd/5th KO, was the son of William and Margaret Ann. He was born in Portinscale, Keswick, enlisted at

Tombstone for Robert Tyson and his wife Sarah Jane (Cowperthwaite) at Crosthwaite Churchyard. The round disc in the middle of the cross bears William's name and reads 'He died for Freedom and Honour'.

Penrith and was killed in action. He was buried at Queant Road Cemetery, Buissy, south of the main Arras to Cambrai road.

Brigham old boy Private Gilbert Sewell, 1st Border, son of William Stoddard and Ann Sewell of Otley Road, Keswick was a tea room assistant (1911 Census). He was killed in action on 2 April 1918. He was buried at Oxford Road Cemetery north east of Ypres.

Joseph Sewell , South Lancashire Regiment, was the son of John and Martha Sewell of Lake Road, Keswick. He was killed in action and buried at Anneux British Cemetery to the south of the main road from Cambrai to Bapaume.

Lance-Corporal Edward Wilson Stanley, Queen's Own Royal West Surreys, was killed on 1 September 1916. He was in charge of a Lewis gun at the time and died immediately; he is remembered on the Thiepval Memorial.

Driver William Tyson, Royal Horse Artillery and Royal Field Artillery, son of Sarah and Robert Tyson of King's Arms Hotel, Keswick, was killed on 2 December, 1917 by a shell which exploded on the road beside the team he was driving. Before the war, he had been an apprentice with W Cowperthwaite and Son, Builders. He was buried at Caestre Military Cemetery, midway between the towns of Cassel and

The plaque was crafted by Mr WH Mawson, erected by old girls and boys of Brigham School, and donated to the museum by Alan Hully of Keswick in 1997. *(Author)*

This war memorial window made by the glassmakers Abbott Bros Lancashire, was at The Acorn Bar, Royal Oak Hotel, Keswick and is now at the Keswick Museum and Art Gallery.

Bailleul. It was opened in mid-April 1918 by the Australian Corps and troops of the 9th (Scottish) Division. It was used until September 1918 for the burials of casualties sustained during the German offensive.

The bronze plaque in memory of Brigham Old Boys who fell in the Great War (seventy six old boys are named) moved to the Keswick Museum and Art Gallery, Station Road, when Brigham School on Penrith Road, Keswick closed. Seven old boys named have the surname Hodgson. One man named (column three) is Andrew Saul, born in Keswick, who was orphaned and adopted by his aunt and uncle, Lavinia and Dunglinson Dykes Tyson and whose address in 1915 was Central Road, Blackpool. Saul trained as a tailor, enlisted in the Duke of Lancaster's Yeomanry, Manchester in October 1915, transferred to the 4th South Lancashire Regiment in December 1916, was posted to the 5th Battalion in January 1917, and the 6th Battalion in September 1917. He served in France and Mesopotamia, was hospitalised in Bombay in September 1918 and discharged as no longer fit for war service in February 1919. Saul, who was married to Mary Jenkinson at Crosthwaite in 1916, died at the Victoria Hospital, Blackpool in November 1919.

The memorial is covered as part of the curtilage.

The central image is of Britannia and a soldier and is titled ‘The Shrine of Honour’. The wording states ‘Who goes there?’- ‘I have no name I died for my Country.’ ‘Pass unknown warrior.’The design is taken from a drawing by Bernard Partridge published in *Punch* magazine in 1921 and this is acknowledged in the window. The window also records ‘In honour of the many patrons of this hotel, who made the supreme sacrifice

Du Boulay pew.

The ROH or Book of Remembrance for World War One and World War Two is inside the church building. The book is internally lit and the pages are turned approximately fortnightly.

There is a memorial plaque at St John's Church, Keswick to Captain Robert Halley Knight, 4th Wiltshire Regiment. He was born in the parish and was killed in action in Palestine on 19 September 1918 (Great Offensive, Battle of Samaria). His father, Alex Knight, was a Keswick doctor and they lived at Brundholme Terrace in 1901.

Inside St John's Church is a freestanding du Boulay wooden pew. Major Thomas William Houssemayne du Boulay lived and died in Kent and was descended from French Huguenots. He was 46 when he died, very probably from the effects of war. He had been a soldier pre-war and was in Burma in 1913 when his son, Joscyln Fogan Houssemayne, was born. Josclyn's uncle Captain Henry Askew, 2nd Border, was killed in action on 19 December 1914 at Sailly, France and buried by the Germans who, as a tribute to his bravery, inscribed on his cross 'Here lies a brave British officer'. There is a brass plaque to Henry Askew inside the Church of St Andrew, Greystoke.

There is a memorial in the form of a slate dedication plaque to Brigham old boy Private George Banks Wivell, 20th Royal Fusiliers, of Keswick at Fitz Park, Station Road, Keswick. The inscription is as follows:

Keswick Hotel, May 1935: The proprietors were the Wivells.

Cambrin churchyard.

THIS ADDITION OF THE FITZ PARK/WAS GIVEN SEPTEMBER 1923 BY/MR & MRS J.B. WIVELL/OF KESWICK HOTEL AS A MEMORIAL/TO THEIR SON GEORGE BANKS.WHO/WAS KILLED IN ACTION AT/GIVENCHY/APRIL 25TH 1916.AND THEIR DAUGHTER/MARY.WHO DIED DECEMBER 4TH 1918.

George's brother Alec was with him when he died. He was shot by a German sniper and carried to a dressing station behind the lines but the wound proved fatal. Before the war, he had worked as an electrical engineer for the British Westinghouse Company. He was buried at Cambrin Churchyard Extension east of Bethune on the road to La Bassee.

At one time the village of Cambrin housed brigade headquarters but until the end of the First World War, it was only about 800 metres from the front line trenches.

A memorial in Keswick is the organ at the Congregational Church in

Lake Road. The organ itself was removed in 2014, but the associated slate plaque remains. It reads:

'The above Organ was dedicated/to the Glory of God
on Feb 2 1923 and as a Memorial to the soldiers of this Church
who fell in the Great War/1914-1918/
ALLEN F CRAIGEN; GEORGE KENNEDY; JOHN M
MICHAEL; CHARLES M PEARS
EDWARD W STANLEY; JAMES WELSH; HERBERT WHITE;
JOHN YOUDALE

Allen Craigen, 24/27th Northumberland Fusiliers (Tyneside Irish), son of John and Catherine Craigen of Keswick, was a coachbuilder by trade working at Grimsby at the time of his enlistment. He died from injuries on 29 December 1917; he had been in France nearly 12 months.

Brigham old boy Second-Lieutenant Charles Martin Pears, 52 Squadron Royal Flying Corps, was the son of Joseph and Laura Pears of Southey Street, Keswick and was educated at Keswick High School. Pears, training to be a teacher before enlistment, had been with his squadron for four months when he was killed. He was killed in a mid-air collision along with his observer William Hartson, while flying on an artillery observation sortie in RE8 A3546 on 23 November 1917. The *Lancashire Evening Post* of 3 December 1917 reported:

> 'A captain, in a letter of sympathy, states that Lieut. Pears was flying on a cloudy day when his machine and another collided on the edge of a cloud bank. Both machines crashed to the ground in the British lines.'

He was buried in a graveyard near to the aerodrome.

James Welsh, whose parents lived at Maxwelltown House, Church Street, Keswick, was presumed fallen in action in France on 18 November 1916. Brigham old boy Herbert White, 11th Kings Liverpool Regiment, was killed in action on 21 March 1918 and commemorated on the Pozieres Memorial, Somme, which has more than 14,000 casualties of the British and 300 of the South African Forces who have no known grave and

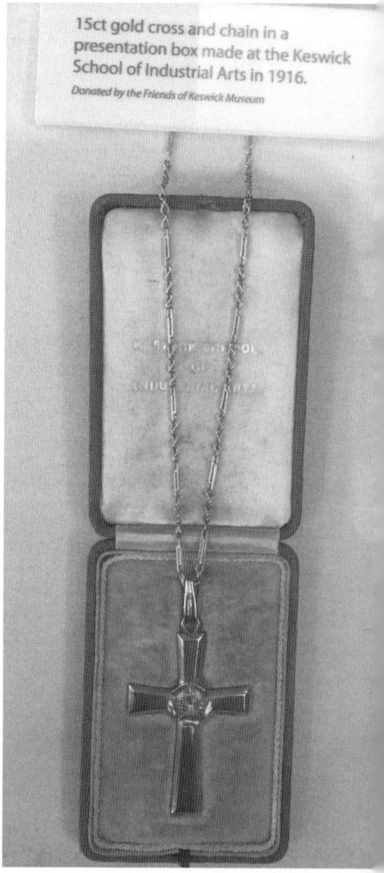

15ct gold cross and chain in a presentation box made at the KSIA in 1916. *(Keswick Muesum)*

The Fretwork War Shrine lay forgotten for many years in a cupboard in the former village school and only saw the light of day in recent years. The workmanship is of high quality.

who died on the Somme from 21 March to 7 August.

Keswick's School of Industrial Art (KSIA) was founded in 1884 by Hardwicke Rawnsley as an evening class in woodwork and repousé metalwork, and swiftly developed a reputation for high quality decorative items made from copper and silver.

The outbreak of the First World War brought dramatic changes as the craftsmen enlisted, and hardship reduced the demand for Arts and Crafts. In these difficult circumstances the School existed by filling a need for memorial plaques and crosses. It could well be that the small Fretwork War Shrine, High Wray, Windermere was created by a local person who had learned the craft of woodworking under Rawnsley. The workmanship is of high quality suggesting a trained hand. An example of a war memorial designed by KSIA is at Dacre, a small village near Penrith, bearing fifteen names. It has clean and formal lines with little embellishment and the letters are created in repoussé.

The Keswick School war memorial was in the old school building of Rawnsley Hall, Keswick. It is now in Queens Hall, Queen Elizabeth Assembly Hall, Keswick. There are thirty names on the memorial.

There was a First World War memorial at Keswick Congregational Church, an organ with a slate plaque below. The organ itself was removed in 2014 as it was never used. The plaque below remains. Eight men are named.

A war memorial window that was at The Acorn Bar, Royal Oak Hotel, Keswick is now at the Keswick Museum and Art Gallery.

Chapter 12

War memorials in surrounding areas

Above Derwent – The unveiling of Above Derwent War Memorial took place at Braithwaite Bridge at 3pm on 5 August 1921. It names nineteen men.

Applethwaite – The Underskiddaw, Applethwaite & Millbeck First World War memorial is beside Underskiddaw Church Rooms, Applethwaite, Keswick. This Celtic-style slate cross was erected in the memory of the four men of Underskiddaw who gave their lives, and also in honour of all who served from the parish and returned; nineteen men. Thomas Bennet Postlethwaite, Merchant Navy, of Brookside, Applethwaite, died when SS *Daybreak*, loaded with iron ore, was sunk as a result of a torpedo fired without warning by *U-87* on Christmas Eve 1917 near South Rock Lightship, Strangford Lough, Co Down with the loss of twenty-one of her crew. On the same day, UK cargo ship *Canova*

Celtic-style cross on two-stepped base.

was torpedoed and sunk twenty-eight kilometres south of Mine Head, Ireland with the loss of seven crew. SS *Daybreak*, built in 1911, lies one mile east of South Rock and is slowly collapsing.

Bassenthwaite – There is a memorial to the local dead of the First World War, with fifteen names outside St John's Church, Bassenthwaite. The Bassenthwaite ROH is inside the church in a glazed wooden frame. Forty-eight men are named; thirty nine served and returned and nine died

Private Richard Corfield, King's Own (KO), from Nuneaton but originally from Bassenthwaite, died within two minutes of his brother, Lance Corporal William Corfield, KO, of Bassenthwaite in the same trench in Ypres on 8 May 1915. The soldier brothers were the sons of Alfred Corfield of North Row, Bassenthwaite,

Applethwaite memorial.

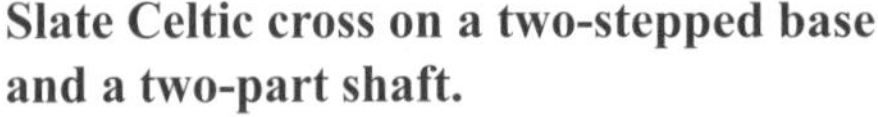

Slate Celtic cross on a two-stepped base and a two-part shaft.

who was for many years a gardener at Armathwaite Hall, Keswick.

Henry Rathbone Hele-Shaw has a memorial at Bassenthwaite St John Church signed Morris & Co. Although his parents, Dr Henry Selby and Mrs Ella Hele-Shaw, lived in London, the memorial is probably here because his mother's family lived at Bassenfell Manor, a country house overlooking Bassenthwaite Lake that was built in 1842 as a country residence for William Rathbone's family. The Rathbones were devout Quakers. Educated at Marlborough, Henry Rathbone had just obtained a scholarship to Clare College, Cambridge when war broke out. He joined the Public Schools Brigade and quickly obtained a commission in the Royal Garrison Army (RGA) and obtained a Royal Aero Club flying certificate number 1728 on 7 September 1915 flying a Maurice Farman biplane. He joined the Royal Flying Corps in late 1915 acting as a ferry pilot before joining 70 squadron where he was very soon wounded. Shortly after rejoining his squadron he got into a scrap while piloting a Sopwith 1½ Strutter A386, with 2nd Lt Robert Claude Oakes (formerly Royal Field Artillery) as observer. On the same day, Ltn Kurt Wintgens of KEK

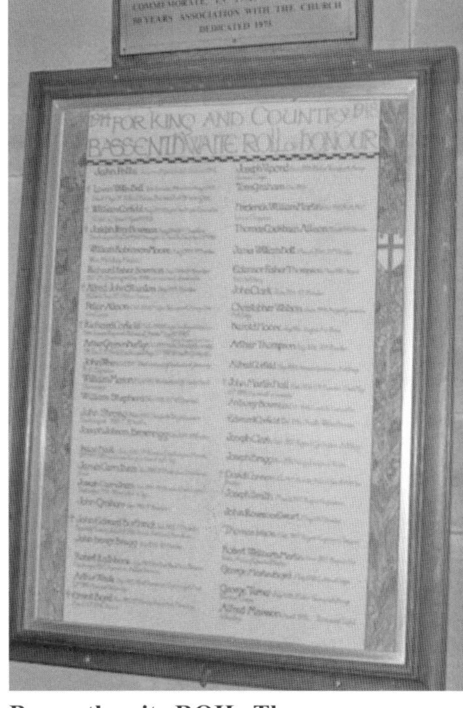

Bassenthwaite ROH . The names are in two columns and are arranged by date of enlistment

Certificate: His date of death here refers to when missing officially became killed.

1728.

SHAW, Henry Rathbone Hele-
64, Victoria Street, S.W.

Born 7th Aug. 1895 *at* Liverpool
Nationality British
Rank, Regiment, Profession 2nd Lieut. R.G.A.
Certificate taken on Maurice Farman Biplane
At Military School, Farnborough
Date 7th September 1915
Killed 18th April, 1917

Arthur Wayman Edwards in the First World War.

Vaux claimed a victory over Strutter '9653' near Arras, probably Hele-Shaw. It was Wintgens' ninth of his eventual nineteen victories. He was shot down on 25 September 1916, aged 20. It seems that Henry was identified and buried by the Germans in the village of Le Verguier near St. Quentin, where his grave was discovered by advancing British troops in April 1917. Post-war, he was reinterred at Jeancourt Communal Cemetery, near Peronne.

Colonel Arthur Wayman Edwards fought in both world wars. Following the death of his wife after he retired to Keswick, he married the widow of Dennis Wivell, the owner of the Keswick Hotel, and lived at Ladstock, Bassenthwaite. In the First World War, Edwards – when a second lieutenant – was wounded twice on the Somme but returned to the front for a third time. He was awarded the Military Cross.. Seaman Dennis Wivell served on *President II* during the war.

Borrowdale has a memorial in the form of a cross at St Andrew's Churchyard in the hamlet of Stonethwaite, below the Borrowdale Fells. It is in memory of six men.

The Borrowdale First World War internal memorial, a wooden board with a statue of a soldier at the centre, is at St Andrew's Church. Ten men of the parish of Borrowdale are listed.

Borrowdale internal memorial.

Edward Leyland, Royal Engineers, who was a partner of Rigg Head slate quarry (on the way up to High Spy from Rosthwaite, Borrowdale) with his brothers, died of wounds at West Vleteren, Belgium on 17 October 1917 and is buried at Dozingham Cemetery, Belgium. He married Mabel Maud Mildred Bownass (1884-1963) in Windermere in 1909 and in 1916 lived at Langstrath, Borrowdale, Keswick. He is also named on the Castle Crag memorial, a dedicatory slate tablet set into a rock, though he is incorrectly spelt as Layland. Mabel ran the Borrowdale Hotel, Keswick after her father (who was the proprietor of the George Hotel, Keswick) bought it in 1926. Leyland enlisted on 10 January 1916 and there was a memo put in with his enlistment form that he should immediately be promoted to Sergeant, and a second memo stating that he was a smart, intelligent quarry manager, a thoroughly competent tunneller. It was just twenty-two days before he was sent to the front, although he had two six-day spells in hospital in 1916. On 5 July 1917, he was promoted to Temporary Second Lieutenant with 175th Tunneling Company. Clearly the Army recognised an asset when they saw one. Rigg Head slate quarry was operational from the late 1880s until its closure in 1934. The range of tasks undertaken by the Royal Engineers during the war was vast, including railway construction and operation, bridge building, barrack building, trench maintenance and repair, searchlight operation, balloon flying, mining, and deploying gas.

John Henry Dover, 11th Border, son of Rueben Dover, is remembered on his father's gravestone at St Andrew's. He was born in Borrowdale, was one of eleven children, and died of wounds in France aged 22.

Prior to enlisting, E.J Boow, Border, had worked for Mr Leyland at the Borrowdale quarries. He died on 1 July 1916 and is buried at Dantzig Alley Cemetery, Mametz.

Private Thomas Richardson, 6th Border, son of John and Mary of Seathwaite, Borrowdale, was a shepherd before the war. He died at Etaples Hospital of German measles and acute bronchitis on 31 March 1917, aged 31, and is buried at Etaples Military Cemetery.

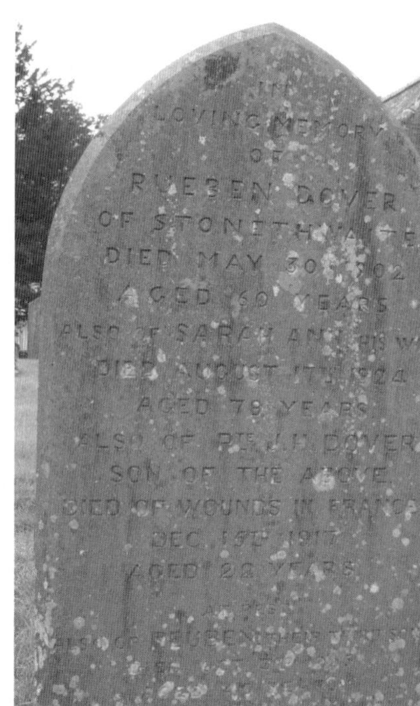

John Henry Dover.

The Borrowdale roadside ROH.

The Men of Borrowdale roadside ROH – a slate plaque set into a wall – is on the B5289 approximately 100 yards south of the vicarage, Stonethwaite, Borrowdale. It records thirty-nine names 'of those in this parish who went forth to the Great War'; twenty-nine served and returned; ten died. Two named on the ROH have the surname Ashworth, two Boow (an unusual surname of Anglo-Saxon original), three Bird, two Brown, two Dover, two Edmondson, five Jenkinson, two Richardson, three Rigg, and two Smith.

Braithwaite – The tapestry inside St Herbert's Church, Braithwaite names nine men and Sarah Barnes. Private James Duffield, 7th Battalion Norfolk Regiment, was the fourth son of the late James and Annie Elizabeth Duffield. He was educated at Keswick School and later learned the trade of joiner under Mr Hunter, Braithwaite. He was killed by heavy shellfire in the advance from Pozieres to Somme on

The tapestry inside St Herbert's Church, Braithwaite.

James Park.

18 August 1916. There is a slate plaque on the front of the Braithwaite & Thornthwaite Victory Memorial Hall, Braithwaite.

Private James Park, was born in Braithwaite to parents Barwise and Sarah and moved to Consett in County Durham at the age of eight. He enlisted in the Coldstream Guards in Newcastle and in August 1914 he was based at Aldershot, before transferring to Chelsea Barracks. He was often on sentry duty at Buckingham Palace. His great-niece Margaret Nesbitt has said:

> 'Here, the sandy ground played havoc with some of his clothes. He used to hang his busby [sic] out of the barracks window overnight to get rid of the sand – and took his sandy socks home on leave for his mother to wash.'

On 13 August 1914, at the age of 21, he landed at Le Havre and probably fought at Mons and Le Cateau before he was wounded. He was treated at La Soupir farmhouse, which was turned into a field hospital to treat casualties. The hospital was bombed on September 17, killing the wounded inside, including Park. He is commemorated on the war memorial at La Ferte-sous-Jouarre in Seine et Marne. La Ferte-sous-Jouarre commemorates nearly 4,000 officers and men of the BEF who died in August, September and the early part of October 1914 and who have no known grave.

Braithwaite Institute – a village hall at the west end of the village of Braithwaite – is a Memorial Hall (with adjacent recreation ground) built by the local community to commemorate victory in the First World War, and is the responsibility of the Hall Management Committee. There is a slate plaque (no names) on the front wall to the right (or east) of the main entrance door of the village hall. It reads Thornthwaite-Cum-Braithwaite/Victory Memorial/1927, and the village hall was opened on 16 November 1927 by RJ Holdsworth, with a golden key. The makers of the hall were Mr Peascod, architect, Messrs I&R Hodgson of Keswick, builder, Messrs Green of Keswick, joiner, Messrs Walker & Son of Keswick, plumber, Mr T Brown of Keswick, painter, and Mr C Forsyth of Keswick. The recreation ground was purchased from Lord Leconfield for less than its agricultural value. Originally it had a bowling green, tennis and croquet courts. In the 1970s, the Thornthwaite and Braithwaite bypass was built on the bed of the old railway, leaving the hall on the other side of a busy road. However, the hall is still very well used, and an integral part of the village.

Brigham – Brigham Memorial Hall was built to commemorate World War One on land given by Maryport Co-operative Society. It was opened on 20 November 1924 by Mr BP Weatherston, ex-serviceman of the

Brigham war memorial.

village. On 9 March 1921, the *West Cumberland Times* reported that a monumental granite cross was unveiled in the grounds of St Bridget's Church, Brigham, a village near Cockermouth that once had a railway station. Twenty-two men are listed.

On 8 June 1915, a crowd of around 3-4,000 gathered at Brigham churchyard for the internment of Private Thomas Parker, 5th Border. He had died at Netley Hospital the previous Saturday of the effects of gas and shrapnel wounds.

Buttermere – The village of Buttermere takes its name from the adjacent lake. Beyond the village of Buttermere is the lake's twin, Crummock Water. The small church of St James contains the region's Roll of Honour.

Caldbeck – The Caldbeck Churchyard Cross is at St Kentigern's Churchyard, Caldbeck and was unveiled in 1922. Seven men are named. Thirty of the fifty names on the Caldbeck ROH in the porch at St Kentigern's Church were natives of the parish and include four sons of John Graves; William, Alfred, John and Frank – all born at Hesket Hall. George Richardson Royal Engineers, and Private Isaac Dickinson Gate. KO, are listed as served and returned, and no less than four Asbridges served and returned – John Samuel P, William Ernest and Tom. The Roll of Honour names three more casualties than the churchyard cross: John

ROH, St James Church. It names seven men and was the gift of Mr and Mrs Nowell Richardson; six men served and returned

Blackley, Robert Jackson and Joseph Yeomans. The five most common surnames in Caldbeck at the time of the UK census of 1881 were (in order of incidence) Scott, Jackson, Richardson, Hodgson, and Bell.

James Chapman of Caldbeck was known for his rhymes that were supposed to express the thanks of the War Office to the parish for its patriotic response to the call for men.

My dear old friends at Caldbeck,

The paper ROH in a three-panel glazed wooden frame. Eighty-five men are named; seventy-five served and returned

Accept my warmest thanks
For the nice young lads you've sent
To join Lord Kitchener's ranks.
I marvel at their smartness,
Which would credit any town,
I never thought that Caldbeck
Could send a 'Bertie Brown.'

As time goes on, dear comrades,
I'll want the ranks to swell,
But you've done your bit in Caldbeck
With Joe and Willie Bell.

The Germans say our Army
Is nothing but a myth,
But they'll alter their opinion
When we send out Private Smith.

We'll drive them into Berlin
Like coneys in a net,
For only a splendid army now,

Including Ted Prim Ett.

There's Gwordie Mark, a good old pal,
Who left his work at school
And as he came I heard him saying
'remember Hartlepool!'

And then there's Georgie Richardson
A lad known far and near;
He'll keep the Allies to the front
And Germans to the rear.

They've robbed and burned and plundered,
Done everything that's bad,
But they've not begun to reckon yet
With Johnnie Thorburn's lad.

We shall wage this war to a finish,
We mean to see it through,
And could you send a few more lads
Like Edgar Asbridge's two?

If they should join the Lonsdales,
Their lot with them to throw,
They'll mate with Gwordie Dobson,
Who comes from Ratten Row
Urge them to join the Army
Before it be too late.
If they can't come with Winter lads,
Then come with Isaac Gate.

And when the war is over
Caldbeck will laud their sons
Who sacrificed 'Home Comforts'
And went to fight the 'Huns.'

Castle Sowerby – There is a War Memorial and an ROH at St Kentigern's Church, Castle Sowerby. On the Castle Sowerby Cross within the churchyard are three names: Corporal John George Trimble, 8th Border, Gunner James Bowes, Royal Horse Artillery and Royal Field

Castle Sowerby church. *(Visit Cumbria).*

The Castle Sowerby Cross

Artillery and Private Thomas Stobart, Norfolk Regiment. Trimble died on 5 July 1916 and is listed on the Thiepval Memorial. Stobart, who died on 6 October 1918, was the son of Thomas and Jane of Sebergham, Dalston, Carlisle. He is buried at Landrecies Communal Cemetery, France. Twenty-one men are named on the ROH; eighteen served and returned.

Cockermouth – The cenotaph, a freestanding memorial to The First World War, listing 132 names with additions for the Second World War, is outside the entrance to the Fire Station headquarters (formerly the railway station), Station Road, Cockermouth. It is a rectangular sandstone column surmounted by a bronze winged figure of victory holding out a wreath. Inside Christ Church, Gallowbarrow, Cockermouth is a framed ROH; 132 men are named (First World War). It is in St Peter's Chapel in the church,and was installed in 1960. The inscription reads: 'This chapel is dedicated to the memory of the men & women of this town who died in the two Wars. Let those who come after see to it that their names be not forgotten.' The Isel Parish ROH is a stone of remembrance at St Michael and All Angels Church, Isel, Cockermouth. A brass plaque inside All Saints Church, Cockermouth was the gift of the Mothers Union 'in memory of this town killed in the Great War'.A marble plaque commemorating the sacrifice of local men in World War One that was originally located in the TocH (an international charitable movement originating from a World War One soldiers' club) building in Cockermouth is now in Cumbria's Museum of Military Life.The most common surnames in Cockermouth at the time of the

Crosthwaite Church viewed from the direction of Portinscale.

UK census of 1881 (in order of incidence) were Robinson, Bell, Thompson, Hodgson, Wilson, Scott, Wilkinson, Jackson, Johnston, and Holmes.

Crosthwaite – A memorial service for the fallen of Keswick and Crosthwaite was held at the parish church of St Kentigern, Crosthwaite on 11 September 1918 and included the names of those who fell. A Great War memorial – a copper plaque on oak backboard – was unveiled by the Bishop of Barrow on 27 August 1922 and is inside the building; fifty-four men are listed. The present current church organ dates from 1920 the original, dating from 1837 was rebuilt and enlarged. It is dedicated to the men of Crosthwaite who died in the Great War.

On 26 September 1924, copper memorial vases were placed next to

The World War One memorial was originally in the belfry but at an early unknown date was moved to its current location on the north wall.

the Church Memorial in the belfry in memory of Frank Gardiner and Richard Usher, KO, son of John and Jane of Albert Street, Millom, two fallen ringers, by their families. The two vases are not on regular display.

Midshipman Douglas Durrant, who was born in Watford and is remembered on the Portsmouth Naval Memorial, was the brother of the curate of Crosthwaite. He died of wounds incurred when HMS *Queen Mary* was sunk on 6 June 1916. She was hit twice by the German battle-cruiser *Derfflinger* during the early part of the Battle of Jutland and her magazines exploded shortly afterwards, sinking the ship. Her wreck was discovered in 1991 and rests in pieces, some of which are upside down, on the floor of the North Sea. *Queen Mary* is designated as a protected place under the Protection of Military Remains Act 1986 as it is the grave of 1,266 officers and men.

Lieutenant Percy Ogden, Royal Flying Corps, husband of Eleanor Jane of Fellside, Manisty, Keswick, died at a military hospital on 7 June 1917. He was the son of Thomas and Jean Edith Ogden of Liverpool. He buried at St Kentigern churchyard (though he is not on the Crosthwaite war memorial).

Eaglesfield, Blindbothel & Mosser – has as the parish memorial a marble plaque, attached to Paddle School near Cockermouth, and commemorates the eight parish men who gave their lives and the thirty-six men who served and returned. Of those who served and returned, three have the surname Clague and five have the surname Harrison.There is a freestanding granite memorial at Eaglesfield Churchyard in memory of the men who gave their lives in both World Wars.

Embleton – the plaque inside St Cuthbert's Church in the small village of and civil parish of Embleton, which abuts the shores of Bassenthwaite Lake, is a bronze plaque on wood backing in memory of three men: Thomas Cecil Beck, North Staffordshire Regiment, Alfred Edmund Watson, 44th Canadian Regiment, and Robinson Watson, 1st Kings Liverpool Regiment. The Embleton Cross in the churchyard is on a two-step base and names the same three men and John Marston, the World War Two casualty, who is buried at Setmurthy. The framed paper Embleton and

This Bible belonged to Private Frederick Peil, 5th Border, from Ireby, north of Keswick. It still has a German machine gun bullet embedded in it.

In memory of the men of Grange-in-Borrowdale who lost their lives in the First and Second World Wars; four men are named.

Wythop ROH with the writing in calligraphy is inside St Cuthbert's. At the top is a picture of warships, a soldier and a lion. Below are the names of the six fallen, then the names of those forty men who served and returned. Three of the deceased are from Embleton, the other three are from Wythop.

In Cumbria's Museum of Military Life is a bronze plaque from the old Wesleyan Chapel in Embleton. It commemorates local men who fought and died in the Great War. Also in the museum is a First World War pocket New Testament Bible. Bibles were often given to soldiers by private individuals, national figures, religious organisations and groups, to comfort them on active service.

Grange-in-Borrowdale – Holy Trinity Church, a chapel of ease, is in the village of Grange-in-Borrowdale. On the outside of the church is a Celtic cross war memorial that has WE Dover on it (Driver William Edward (Ted) Dover). His grave is at St Andrews church in the hamlet of Stonethwaite three miles away. A chapel of ease was provided for the convenience of parishoners who lived some distance from the main parish church. Marriages, Christenings and other services could be performed in these chapels but few enjoyed the rights of burial.

A tablet was erected on the top of Castle Crag, according to the *Penrith Observer* on 21 June 1921. The Castle Crag dedicatory slate tablet set into a rock reads:

'Castle Crag was given to the
National Trust in Memory Of
John Hamer
2nd Lieut 6th KSLI born July 8 1897
killed in action March 22 1918
Also of/the following men of Borrowdale
who died for the same cause/'

Castle Crag dedicatory slate tablet. The first name is John Hamer.

Granite Celtic style cross: This First and Second World War memorial is in St James' Churchyard in the village of Ireby and lists seven names for 1914-1918.

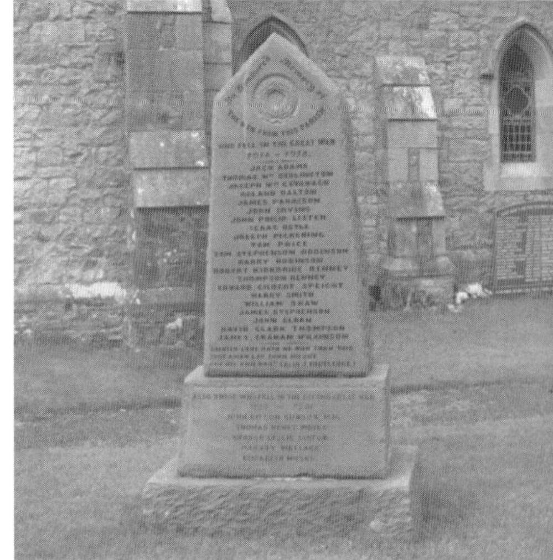

Slate stone on a two stage base.

There are eleven names. John Hamer King's Shropshire Light Infantry, was not local but from north-west London. Initially the monument was only to be for Hamer, but his parents, Sir William – a London doctor – and Lady Agnes, were persuaded by Hardwicke Rawnsley to add the local men as well, although there was already a memorial to them in Grange-in-Borrowdale churchyard. Sir William bought Castle Crag and gave it to the National Trust in 1920.

Great and Little Broughton – There is a freestanding First and Second World War memorial in the churchyard in the village of Great Broughton near Cockermouth with twenty-one names. There is also a ROH in the British Legion Club.

Ireby – The Ireby paper ROH with twenty-seven names and calligraphic text is set in a dark wooden frame with gold-coloured edging. Twenty men served and returned. It was in the Wesleyan Methodist Chapel in the village until the chapel closed and was funded from the surplus for the external memorial. It is now in St James' Church. Three men have the surname Lorrimer: Balfour, David and

Ireby ROH inside St James' Church, west end of north wall.

John. At St James' Church is a Celtic cross unveiled on 12 June 1921. There are seven First World War names on the memorial. The gravestone of Robert Wood is near the vestry door. Wood, son of Wilson and Elizabeth, joined the Canadian Army and died at the Battle of the Somme on 2 October 1916. He was 466370 of 5th Battalion Canadian Infantry and his father lived at Aughertree, so he appears to have been omitted from the Ireby memorial in error. He is not on any local war memorial.

Lamplugh – There is a First and Second World War memorial, a granite cross, in St Michael's Churchyard in the scattered community and civil parish of Lamplugh bearing thirty names for World War One

George Fryer Dickinson.

and four for World War Two.There is a Dickinson Brothers brass plaque in St Michael's: Captain Ronald Dickinson was killed in action near Hooge on 16 June 1915; Captain Alan Peile Dickinson was killed in action at Le Plantin on 1 June 1918. They were both in the 10th (Scottish) Battalion, Kings Liverpool Regiment.

Another memorial in St Michael's is to their brother Captain George Fryer Dickinson, 10th (Scottish) Battalion, Kings Liverpool Regiment. He died on 28 May 1932 as a result of wounds and ill-health contracted in the war. The family lived at Red How, Lamplugh.

The Methodist Chapel at Kirkland, Lamplugh re-opened for regular worship in February 1921. A church hall was added in the late Twenties or early Thirties. This hall was in fact a hut originally built for munition workers at Gretna in the First World War. The hut was moved to Kirkland for use at the Barbara Pit but was no longer needed and sold to the chapel trustees.

Little Town – The Newlands School ROH in Newlands Church in the hamlet of Little Town near Keswick is in pre-printed paper form with the thirteen names handwritten in a glazed wooden frame. It was originally in the adjacent schoolroom until that closed.

John Edmondson 1st Border, was the son of John and Dinah of Seathwaite Farm, Keswick and he lived at the Forge, Keswick at the time of enlistment on 10 December 1915. He entered France on 27 July 1916, was wounded in action on 21 October, with shrapnel wounds to his back, abdomen, left wrist and ankle, and was missing, presumed dead, 11-13 April 1918. He is commemorated on Ploegsteert Memorial south of Ypres. Also commemorated on Ploegsteert is Private John Edwards, son of William and Mary of Kings Head Court, Keswick, and Brigham old boy Private Edwin Evans, 8th Border, of 21 Rose Terrace, Keswick, who was killed in action. He was a 'painter on railway'.

Sergeant Lewthwaite Foster, Machine Gun Corps, was the son of Robert and Jane of Keswick and the husband of Hannah of Main Street, Keswick. He worked as a joiner before the war, enlisted on 4 July 1916, arrived in France on 14 December 1916 and was killed in action on 12 October 1917 (France and Flanders). He is buried at Poelcapelle British Cemetery north-east of Ypres.

Private Robert Postlethwaite, before the war, was an auxiliary postman doing the Newlands round. He also worked part-time at Swinside Farm and Derwent Bank. He was killed in action on 28 May 1917 in Gouzeaucourt, France.

Inside Newlands Church is a stained glass window to all who died in World War One as well as Private Thomas Roscoe Johnson, 17th Battalion King's Liverpool Regiment, who was killed in action in France. He was reported as missing since 12 October 1916 and afterwards ascertained to have been killed in action on that date. He was a native of Liverpool. There is a Newlands School First World War ROH in the church.

Inscription: 'In grateful memory of those those who/gave their lives for their country, and rest in unknown graves/and especially of Thomas Roscoe Johnson.'

There is a First World War brass plaque on wooden backboard inside the church in the fairly isolated village of Lorton, four miles from Cockermouth (eleven names).

Alison White Towers, Westmorland & Cumberland Yeomanry, was a banker. He died on 2 October 1916 and was buried at Richbourg-st-Vaaast, France. The Westmorland & Cumberland Yeomanry regiment was formed on the creation of the TF in April 1908 and placed under orders of the Welsh Border Mounted Brigade. It was headquartered at Penrith. The B Squadron Penrith included Keswick, Temple Sowerby and Cockermouth.

Thomas Head, 1st Border, who lived in Brackenthwaite in the Lorton valley, died on 13 August 1915 when the *Royal Edward* troopship was sunk. He is listed on the Helles Memorial, Turkey. RMA (later HMT) Royal Edward was a passenger ship belonging to the Canadian Northern Steamship Company that was sunk by *UB-14* near the island of Kos in the Aegean on 13 August 1915 with a large loss of life while transporting Commonwealth troops. All were destined for Gallipoli. Private John Jackson of Cleator Moor, Cumbria also drowned on *Royal Edward*.

The church dates almost entirely from the year 1884 when a vast expansion in population was predicted because a lead mine was opened at Godferhead, Loweswater. The mine failed and the population remained static.

Long Marton Village Hall – Long Marton is a village and civil parish in the Eden district with a railway station (closed 1970) on the Settle to Carlisle line. The inscription on the ROH is as follows: Roll of Honour/European War 1914-1919/Provided by the Women's War Working Party/Names of those who served in His Majesty's Forces/from LONG MARTON, BRAMPTON AND KNOCK.

Loweswater – The First World War memorial inside St Bartholomew's Church in this village and civil parish is a freestanding timber lectern or desk with incised lettering. It is on its original site and is in memory of five men.

Matterdale – There are two simple marble plaques to the fallen on the inside wall of the church here, a civil parish that runs the length of a valley from the main Penrith to Keswick road to Ullswater. The First World War tablet is in memory of five men.

Patterdale is a small village and civil parish by Ullswater and Helvellyn. The Patterdale ROH in the village hall names 103 men who

Beneath is a plain white marble tablet listing the names of the two men who lost their lives in World War Two.

served in World War One; ninety-one served and returned. Towards the end of the First World War, the inhabitants of the parish collected money in order to establish a permanent monument as a memorial to the fifteen officers and men who fell in the Great War. In February 1921, William Hibbert Marshall, owner of Patterdale Hall, donated a piece of land adjacent to the A592 near St Patrick's Well to allow for the building of a permanent monument. The memorial slab was unveiled on 20 October 1921. The very first name on the memorial is G.R Bennett and has long been a mystery to researchers. In January 1915, Mrs Marshall of Patterdale Hall compiled a list of parishioners serving in Her Majesty's Forces, published in three local newspapers. The *Westmorland Gazette* listed a Private P.G Bennett, East Yorks. The *Cumberland & Westmorland Herald* listed him as Private G.P Bennett, East Yorks. The

The memorial slab was hewn from a 20 ton piece of local slate.

Penrith Observer listed him as Private Grenville Bennett, East Yorkshire.

Second on the list is Private Frank Brown the eldest son of David Brown, a lead miner, and his wife Mary Jane (nee Dewis). After leaving Patterdale School, he initially worked – at the age of fourteen – as a lead ore washer at the Greenside Mine but later worked as a farm labourer at Edenhall, Penrith. He went to Penrith on 11 February 1915 and signed up to join the 2nd/4th Border Regiment. On 4 March 1915, the battalion of twenty-eight officers and 767 other ranks left Avonmouth docks on board HM Troopship (HMT) *Dongola* bound for Bombay, India. Running at night without lights because of U-boats, the ship collided with a steamer in the Bristol Channel just off Barry and everyone had to be quickly landed ashore. A replacement ship was found and departed from Barry on 7 March, passing through the Mediterranean and the Suez Canal before reaching Bombay on the morning of 31 March. Their final destination was the Ghorpuri Barracks, Pune, India. Whilst serving in India, Brown would have served in Shankargarh, Nowshera, Peshawar and Sadar Garhi (for service on the Mohmand Blockade line in response

Platoon No 6 of B Company 2nd/4th Border Regiment whilst in India.

to Mohmand attacks). He is known to have suffered a short bout of malaria in October 1916 and a more prolonged bout in September 1918 whilst in Nowshera. Upon returning to Peshawar, presumably still in a weakened state, he contracted influenza and was admitted to the hospital there on 21 October. His condition worsened and he died on Wednesday 30 October 1918, aged 22. He is buried at Peshawar. The Mohmand blockade (1916-17) was a series of defences by the Indian Army during World War One. The Mohmands submitted in July 1917.

Private Frederick Kirkland, before the outbreak of war, got a job driving the mail motor bus which Messrs Taylor Motors Ltd ran between Penrith and Patterdale. Probably in response to posters such as 'Motor Drivers Required For the Army Service Corps', he enlisted in Penrith early in the war and joined the Mechanical Transport section of the Army Service Corps. He arrived in France on 16 July 1915. Before he died of wounds on 31 March 1918, he was an ambulance driver with the 43rd Field Ambulance (Royal Army Medical Corps).

Glenridding Memorial Cottage was built of local Lakeland stone to commemorate the First World War. In 1921, the residents of Patterdale raised £100 (by donation and subscription) to purchase a cottage house that not only would become a permanent memorial but also a local home. 'for the benefit of inhabitants of the Parish of Patterdale in Perpetuity,' in the words of the 1921 Indenture. It was known as Nurses' Cottage and occupied iniitally by a district nurse named Maggie Paull. Westmorland County Council paid the annual rent which commenced at £6 per year. At the time, the district nurse lived within the parish to support the population that included the families of those who worked in Greenside Mine. Alice Rebecca Banks, a nurse who was born in Newcastle-upon-Tyne, lived at The Cottage House in the 1920s, when it became known as Memorial Cottage. By the time she lived there, she had married (1920) local man Joseph Greenhow, a miner at Greenside and First World War veteran (Private Joseph Greenhow, 1st Border). Memorial Cottage ceased to be a home for the District Nurse in 1965 as there was no longer a need for a nurse to live within the parish.

A local man who served during the Gallipoli campaign was Ernest James Plummer, who was born in Watermillock. He enlisted with the Royal Navy in 1912, age 16, and joined HMS *Hibernia* in January 1914 as an able seaman, and remained on board until the end of September 1915. During that period, his ship supported the Dardenelles campaign and provided cover for the evacuation from the Gallipoli peninsula. A

St Barnabas' Church, Setmurthy: There are several stained glass windows worth looking at, all being monuments to the Fisher family of Higham Hall, Bassenthwaite Lake.

year later, he came under German fire during the Battle of Jutland. He died in London in 1962.

Another local man involved in the Gallipoli campaign was Dawson Bowman, who was baptised at Patterdale Church on 7 November 1880. He was the son of Joe "Hunty" Bowman, huntsman of the Ullswater Foxhounds. Dawson Bowman started as a Battery Quarter Master Sergeant in the Royal Field Artillery (RFA) and gained promotion to Lieutenant in the Royal Garrison Artillery, on 15 June/23 July 1915, and then was made a captain in the RFA. He served in the Mediterrean Expeditionary Force (MEF) who were involved in the ill-fated Gallipoli campaign, and he was also based in Egypt. Dawson Bowman and his wife initially returned to Patterdale.

In memory of Dorothy Fisher of Higham: Two light stained glass window by Abbot of Lancaster depicting St George & St Dorothea.

Higham Hall was built about 1800. There are four acres of informal Victorian gardens.

Setmurthy – Inside the church is a brass plaque 'in loving memory of those connected with this parish who made the supreme sacrifice in the Great War'. It names two men and nurse Dorothy Fisher, British Red Cross. Her father was Joseph Fisher of Higham Hall, Bassenthwaite Lake, whose money had come from a marriage into a shipping family in the North East, transporting coal to London.

St John's in the Vale – High on the western side of the vale is St John's in the Vale Church. There is an external memorial, a stone of remembrance, to the ten dead of the Great War. There is an ROH inside the church, a large red marble plaque with fifty-five names. Three have the surname Harding. At the church on 12 August 1916, there was a memorial service for Private John Moffat Bragg – the £3 offertory to be used towards the eventual memorial tablet to all from the church lost in the war – this is very early for such a collection.

Threkeld is a village and civil parish about four miles east of Keswick that formerly had its own railway station on the CK & PR. Until 1982, Threlkeld was an important centre of mining and quarrying.

The Threlkeld First World War ROH, in a glazed wooden frame, is inside the village hall

Simple unfashioned slate stone of remembrance.

and lists ninety-one names. Of the casualties listed, Birkett Stuart, Westmorland and Cumberland Yeomanry and 7th Border, Thomas Stuart, 8th Border, and Charles Henry Stuart were brothers. They were the sons of Thomas and Jane of Brooklyn House, Threlkeld. A cousin of these four brothers also lost his life in the First World War. He was James Bowes Stuart, 4th Border, son of Robert and Margaret of the Post Office, Threlkeld. He died in India on 16 November 1918. Three on the ROH have the surname name Airey; three Edwards; three Greenop; three Harding; three Hebson; three Hind; four Hindmoor, three Mills; and four Robinson.

Threlkeld Village Memorial is opposite the old Post Office.

Threlkeld Village Memorial, Stuart Terrace, is in memory of the men of Threlkeld district who died in the World Wars and bears thirteen names for the First War and five for the Second.

The St Mary's Church, Threlkeld First World War memorial is inside the building and commemorates twelve men who died in the Great War. T.A Watson is buried in a war grave in the churchyard but he is omitted from this memorial. He died on 14 November 1918. There is a brass memorial to Lieutenant Caradoc Stuart McLeod Prinsep inside St Mary's, erected by his aunt Audrey C Howard. He was born in Egypt, lived in London, and one of thirty men lost on *G7* when communication was lost with her base at Blyth on 23 October 1918. He was the son of Captain James F.M Prinsep, Essex Regiment, who attended Charterhouse and was an English footballer. Most sources record that he was killed fighting in Egypt in 1895. It is not known what happened to *G7* or even the location of the wreck in the North Sea. She was declared formally lost with all hands on 1 November 1918.

Richard Burrow Hodgwin, who did national service on the East coast during the Great War, was a stonemason who carved Threlkeld War Memorial. According to the *Keswick Reminder* on 21 November 1924, he offered himself for service in but was refused because he was too old.

Underskiddaw – The war memorial in the civil parish of

Underskiddaw war memorial.

Underskiddaw, immediately north of Keswick, was 'erected in memory of the men … of Underskiddaw who gave their lives for country and for freedom' –and 'also in honour of those who served from this parish in the war' – this section has nineteen names.

Inside the church is a paper handwritten ROH, dated 1 March 1918, in a glazed wooden frame. There are twenty-three names on this memorial; nineteen men served and returned.

There is a memorial inside St John's Church, Hensingham, Whitehaven, a wooden board with writing in gold paint on its original site, to the memory of the twelve members of the Cumberland Change Ringers Association who fell in the Great War. There are names from Cleator Moor, Keswick, Carlisle, Cockermouth and Workington. The act of dedication was the ringing of the peal itself on 6 May 1922.

Chapter 13

Railwaymen Remembered

One hour after war was declared, the Railway Executive Committee took over the railways and kept control until 15 August 1921. The first major task was the mobilisation of the armed forces. Another major role for the country's railways was in bringing and taking goods from munitions factories. An instruction was issued in February 1915 that railwaymen were not to be accepted into the armed forces without a signed certificate from their local management effectively agreeing to their volunteering for service. Nevertheless, by the first anniversary of the start of the war, well over ten per cent of those who were railwaymen in August 1914 were now to be found in the army or the navy. By October 1916, the railways nationally had released 119,600 men for military service, but about as many men had also left for other essential work, including the manufacturing of munitions. By Armistice Day, 184,475 men from the railway companies had entered the armed forces, equal to 49 per cent of the number of railwaymen of military age (18-45) on 4 August 1918.

From the CK & PR, 39 men signed up and seven names are commemorated on the CK&PR war memorial. Some of these railwaymen were not Keswickians by birth or abode. Even so, they

The bronze panel - unveiled by Major Hamlet Riley DL JP LLB, chairman of CK & PR, on 1 May 1920 - was moved from the railway station when it closed

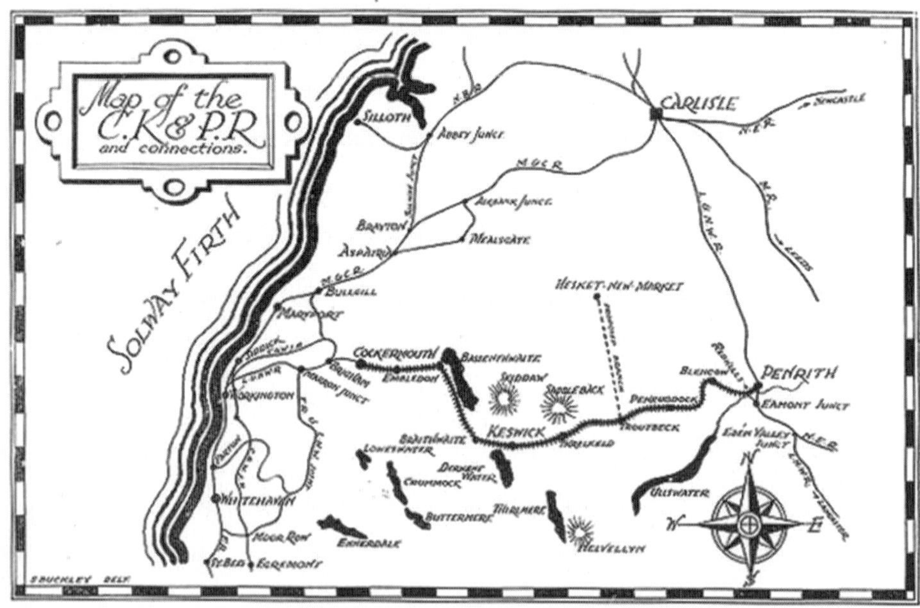

Route map of the CK&PR.

worked on the railways in the area and lived nearby.

The CK & PR First World War bronze plaque was moved from Keswick railway station when it closed. It is now on the south side of Keswick War Memorial. The men named are: Brigham old boy Sergeant William Notman a yardsman at Threlkeld, 4th Border; Brigham old boy Corporal John Youdale, a clerk at Keswick railway station, 2nd Border; Private J John Dixon Gibson, a platelayer 2nd/4thBorder; Private Joseph William Hebson, a signalman at Troutbeck, 5th Border;Private William Park Hetherington, a porter who lived in Cockermouth, 6th Border; Private Martin S Mitchinson, porter 8th Border; and Private Robinson Watson, a porter,1st King's Liverpool Regiment. Notman, of Wordsworth Street, Keswick died at the Somme. He was killed by a shell exploding in the trenches on 21 October 1916.

Keswick railway station on 6 March 1972, the day it closed.

Bassenthwaite Lake Station, June 2007. The CK & PR railway stations from west to east were Cockermouth, Embleton, Basssenthwaite Lake, Braithwaite, Keswick, Threlkeld, Troutbeck (for Ullswater), Penruddock, Blencow and Penrith. There was a halt on the CK&PR for workers at the Briery Bobbin Mill (not a proper station but a raised drop-off point).

George Armstrong , Royal Welsh Fusiliers, is not named. He was the signalman at Bassenthwaite Lake Station. Prior to the war, he was a member of the Cumberland and Westmorland Police. He died in 1918 and is buried at Terlincthun British Cemetery, Boulogne.

Fifty men of the Cleator & Workington Junction Railway joined up

Embleton station 1910: Embleton station closed on 13 September 1958.

and six staff who lost their lives in the war have been identified from staff records and the National ROH. No war memorial erected by the Cleator & Workington Junction Railway has been traced. However, the Cumbrian Railways Association has further details about these men. Sixty-eight employees of the Furness Railway are commemorated on the Furness Railway memorial at Barrow station. Seventeen of the Maryport & Carlisle Railway and twenty of the North Eastern Railway lost their lives. The war memorial of the NER is located in Station Road, York.

The LNWR War Memorial is located in front of Euston railway station in London but there are no names of individuals on the memorial. 31,744 employees of the company served in the armed forces during the First World War; 3,700 died. Seventy railwaymen from Cumbria who worked for LNWR lost their lives. Eight worked at Penrith and seven at Workington.

On 8 March 1915, a train conveying the usual complement of 100 wounded soldiers arrived in Carlisle on its way to Glasgow. The men belonged to various regiments, principally Scottish, and none of them was regarded as a serious case. Amongst the men were the following Cumbrians: Private Dodd, formerly a porter at Penrith Station who had lost the index finger on his left hand blown off by a grenade exploding in his trench; Private Lee, another Penrith man, had a septic ankle; Private Pape of Wigton and Private Battersby of Maryport were invalided for operations; Private Bunty of Cockermouth had an injured knee cartilage requiring an operation.

'The outbreak of the war led to some drastic changes in the railway system in Britain. Trains were the most useful way of moving goods for the war effort as well as men from one place to another. Although the previous few years had been relatively peaceful with regard to the number of accidents and fatalities on the railways, this was all to change,' according to *Britain's Railway Disasters: Fatal Accidents from the 1830s to the Present Day* by Michael Foley. There was a railway catastrophe at Little Salkeld, on the Settle-Carlisle line, on 22 January 1918 when the Scotch Express ran into a landslide. Six lives were lost and many were injured. Three-hundred passengers had a marvellous escape, according to the *Penrith Observer* of 22 January 1918. Private Walter Firth, stationed at Paisley, from Halifax, Yorkshire survived. He had boarded the train at Skipton, Yorkshire and was in one of the wrecked carriages. He was returning to his regiment after special leave. The biggest loss of life in a rail accident in British history happened on Saturday 22 May 1915, at Quintinshill just outside Gretna. Five trains were involved with around 230 people killed. Most of the dead were Royal Scots troops heading to Gallipoli.

Chapter 14

Economising and hunger

Hardwicke Rawnsley, on 23 January 1915, suggested that older children attending public elementary schools and pupils in evening classes in Cumberland should be encouraged to make toys, in view of the failure of the normal supply from the Continent. The Cumberland Education Authority established an experimental class in toy-making at the KSIA in 1916.

On 31 July 1915, the *Cumberland News* gave advice on economising:

> 'All treating should be given up until we can toast to final and complete victory. The real motto should be "No drink till we have won".'

On 11 August 1915, the *Westmorland Gazette* said:

> 'Changes of fashion (one of the greatest causes of extravagant expenditure on dress) should be ignored, if they cannot be suppressed. All not strictly necessary extras, such as veils, white gloves, furs, silk garments, should not be bought. Many women might save quite substantial sums by spending no money on scents, cosmetics, etc, and by avoiding unnecessary visits to the hairdressers and manicurist.'

The 12 September 1915 issue of the *Carlisle Journal* advised women:

> 'It is to be hoped that fantastic, unmeaning and frivolous dressing will be abandoned for more womanly fashions. The serious pursuits women are engaged in now, the voluntary service given by our sex to the State, and the grave aspect of our national affairs in general, not to mention the dread toll of young life paid, must naturally in all but the most frivolous and unfeeling, produce an attitude of mind repellent of folly and extravagance in any form, dress included.'

Unrest and riots broke out in Cumberland in early 1917 when the

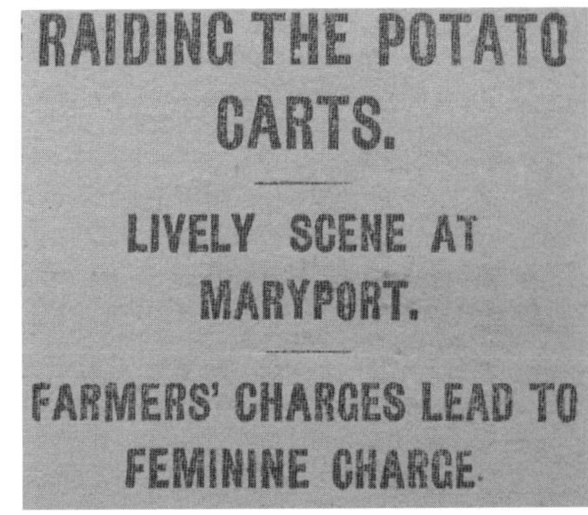
RAIDING THE POTATO CARTS.

LIVELY SCENE AT MARYPORT.

FARMERS' CHARGES LEAD TO FEMININE CHARGE.

Headline news: "Farmers' charges lead to feminine charge"

price of potatoes saw a fourfold increase. In the Maryport Christmas market, a boycott by housewives reduced geese from one and threepence to nine pence per pound, a sixty percent reduction, and the women declared they were ultimately proved as successful with potatoes as with geese. In January 1917, they sent the town crier around to make sure that everybody was united and asking women not to buy but to boycott the cost of potatoes at a ridiculously high price. There was some difficulty; some of the farmers decided they were just going to take their crops home. Others did give in and sell for a shilling to clear their stocks and off they went. Carts were overturned, people were hurt and generally the story spread through the rest of the county. There were disturbances and riots the following week in Carlisle market. In Keswick, there was 'a bit of a do' with two farmers who turned up wanting to market one day, and some soldiers got involved on the side of the housewives, the carts were overturned and the boys in the town were suddenly seen with their caps and their pockets bulging with potatoes as they scurried around trying to pick up as they fell off.

The other fall-out from this was the theft of potatoes. Marian Atkinson grew up in the Lake District and was a 12-year-old schoolgirl in 1917:

> 'We'd see turnips, potatoes and cabbage and we'd decide what we'd pinch on the way home. On the way back, the bigger boys used to say "Keep your eyes rolling for the farmer." My parents wouldn't accept anything stolen – they used to make us take it back – so we used to sit under a hedge and gnaw the vegetables like a rabbit. If we could hear the farmers' horses clip-clopping, we used to bung what we'd been eating under the hedge and go like lightning back home, large as life.'

A list of foods for which maximum retail prices apply was printed in the *Westmorland Gazette* on 8 September 1917: Wheat and all cereals; beef, veal, mutton, lamb, pork; butter, bacon, ham, lard; sugar, cheap tea, cheap coffee; sweets, jams, juices; dried beans, dried peas; herrings, oats, oatmeal, maize foods. Working class families across Britain were helped significantly by the introduction of general food rationing in February 1918. By April, all districts, whether rich or poor, received equal shares of meat and various other foodstuffs. Perhaps, because of its rural situation, a good proportion of the population of Cumberland had a less arduous time with regard to food rationing in World War One than most city dwellers.

The following, from TR Hayes, Vice-chairman, Keswick Urban District Council, was printed in the *Lancashire Evening Post* on 25

January 1918 and entitled *Keswick and Food Production*. He complained that the food producers were sent forward "without compunction", the result being that "not only is there a scarcity of vegetables and prices prohibitive, but acres of good market are going to wreck, infested with weeds".

> 'Sir – Every patriotic person will be at one with the Director-General of National Service when he says that there are in civil life a large number of men holding certificates who are engaged in work of practically no national importance. I am voicing the opinion of a large number of the people of Keswick when I say that we have a most unsatisfactory state of things here. Practically the only men who were of national importance – the food producers, whose services would have been of untold value in tilling and cropping the land – were sent forward without compunction, the result being that not only is there a great scarcity of vegetables and prices prohibitive, but acres of good market and other gardens are going to wreck, and are infested with the worst type of weeds, which are a menace to other cultivated ground.
>
> 'The great hardship to Keswick, not only as a visiting resort, but to the residents, is the utter disregard by the Tribunal for the production of food, while persons who are not doing any work of national importance are exempted. This demands the strictest investigation, and at a crisis like this it should not be necessary to draw attention to such inconsistencies.'

There was an urgent appeal printed in the *Penrith Observer* on 15 January 1918 from the Penrith Gas Works to the Penrith Urban District Council to exert their best endeavours to get householders to save coal: 'Use coke as much as possible in order that coal may be saved for vital National purposes'. The Penrith Rural Control Committee met, according to the *Penrith Observer* on 29 January 1918. Topics up for discussion were butchers' troubles, restrictions on sheep killing, a milk hardship and whether public teas and suppers should be barred. Farmers were urged by the Poultry Advisory Committee to limit the amount of foodstuffs for poulty-feeding, according to the *Penrith Observer* on 5 February 1918. And a report in the *Penrith Observer* on 2 July 1918 stated that less local butter would be made. In the *Penrith Observer* on 27 August 1918, there was an appeal to save on boots and shoes. The first tip from the War Savings Certificates was 'always stand wet boots to dry and the soles uppermost'

Chapter 15

Marking the end of the war

'Keswick received the news of the armistice very quietly but none the less with gladness. The church bells rang out, and shortly afterwards flags were flying from windows and masts which made the town look quite gay. Thanksgiving services were held in the various Churches. At Crosthwaite a united service was well attended. The Rev WE Bradley gave the address. In the service he was assisted by the Rev W Treleaven. At St John's a good congregation assembled, and the Rev GH Lewin conducted the service.'

(*West Cumberland Times* 16 November1918)

The news of the signing of the Armistice reached Caldbeck at midday on Monday November 11 1918. The ringing of the church bells by the parish clerk and the hoisting of the flag on the church tower were to many the first intimation of the good news. On the following Sunday, a solemn Te Deum was sung and services of Thanksgiving held both morning and evening at the parish church, and the proceeds of the collections were given to the Red Cross.

On 7 February 1919, a whist drive and dance was held at Threlkeld for a Peace Treat for the schoolchildren to recognise their work in helping local soldiers. The Keswick Friendly Societies' annual sports on 4 August 1919 attracted a record crowd of 5,000 as reported by the Lancashire Evening Post on 5 August 1919. Attractions included a band contest and the competition for the 11-stone world's wrestling cup. There was good sport throughout. Cockermouth peace celebrations were held at Christ Church and Fairfield School on 19 July 1919. The Keswick Reminder on 15 August 1919 reported that a Flag Day would be held on Saturday 16 August in aid of the Keswick and District Fund for Blinded Sailors and Soldiers and the National Institute for the Blind. And the first annual show of the newly-formed Cockermouth Agricultural Society was held in September 1919.

From page five of the *Cumberland & Westmorland Herald* 16 September 1922, we know that the Lowther churchyard entrance gates (which have no wording nor plaque) in the village of Lowther were war memorial gates, unveiled on 9 July 1922 – the personal gift of the Countess of Lonsdale. Lord Lonsdale unveiled the brass tablet inside the church. The day included trooping of the colour of the 11th Border at the end of its life with 637 survivors of the battalion.

> 'A remembrance service was held at the Keswick War Memorial on Tuesday 11 November 1924. There was a large attendance, including school children, ex-Servicemen, members of Keswick council, and members of Keswick Women's Section of the British Legion. After the two minutes' silence, Bandsman O Rigg sounded the Last Post and the Reveille. The service concluded with prayer and the signing of 'God Save the King'. Many wreaths and other floral tributes were laid at the foot of the memorial, including wreaths from the British Legion, the Women's Legion, the VAD, the Keswick Council, and wreaths of laurel with the centre filled with red poppies pinned thereon by ex-servicemen, and women and children.' (*Lancashire Evening Post*, 12 November 1924).

Appendix 1

Border Regiment actions and movements 1914-18

1st Battalion

4 August 1914: Stationed at Maymyo, Burma at the outbreak of war.
9 December 1914: Embarked for England from Bombay landing at Avonmouth.
10 January 1915: Moved to Rugby to join the 87th Brigade of the29th Division.
17 March 1915: Mobilised for war and embarked for Gallipoli from Avonmouth via Alexandria and Mudros.
25 April 1915: Landed at Gallipoli and engaged in various actions against the Turkish Army.
9 January 1916: Evacuated to Mudros due to heavy casualties from combat, disease and severe weather, and then moved to Alexandria.
March 1916: Moved to France and engaged in various actions on the Western Front including;
During 1916: Albert; Transloy Ridges.
During 1917: First, Second and Third Scarpe; Langemarck; Broodseinde; Poelcapelle; Cambrai.
During 1918: Estaires; Messines; Hazebrouck; Bailleul; Outtersteene Ridge; Ploegsteert and Hill 63; Ypres; Courtrai.
11 November 1918: Ended the war in Belgium near Celles S.W. of Renaix.

2nd Battalion

4 August 1914: Stationed at Pembroke Dock and then moved to Lyndhurst to join the 20th Brigade of the 7th Division.
6 October 1914: Mobilised for war and landed at Zeebrugge and engaged in various actions on the Western Front including;
During 1914: First Ypres.
December 1914: This Battalion took part in the Christmas Truce.
During 1915: Neuve Chapelle; Aubers; Festubert; Givenchy; Loos.
During 1916: Albert; Bazentin; High Wood; Delville Wood; Guillemont; the Ancre.
During 1917: The German retreat to the Hindenburg Line; Arras; Polygon Wood; Broodseinde; Poelcapelle; Second Passchendaele,
November 1917: Moved to Italy to strengthen the Italian resistance.
4 November 1918: Ended the war in Italy, Pozzo east of Pordenone.

3rd (Reserve) Battalion
4 August 1914: Stationed at Carlisle then moved to Shoeburyness.
January 1916: Moved to Conway and then Barrow.
March 1917: Moved to Great Crosby, near Liverpool until the end of the war.

1/4th (Cumberland & Westmorland) Battalion Territorial Force
4 August 1914: Stationed at Carlisle and attached to the East Lancs. Division and then moved to Barrow.
September 1914: Moved to Sittingbourne and transferred to the Middlesex Brigade of the Home Counties Division.
29 October 1914: Embarked for India from Southampton arriving at Rangoon December 1914: Division then broken up and remained in India throughout the war.

1/5th (Cumberland) Battalion Territorial Force
4 August 1914: Stationed at Workington attached to the East Lancs. Division and then moved to Barrow.
26 October 1914: Mobilised for war and landed at Le Havre to defend the Lines of Communication.
5 May 1915: Transferred to 149th Brigade of the 50th Division.
20 December 1915: Transferred to 151st Brigade of the 50th Division and continued to engage in various actions on the Western Front including;
During 1915: St Julien; Frezenburg Ridge; Bellewaarde Ridge.
During 1916: Flers-Courcelette; Morval; Transloy Ridges.
During 1917: First Scarpe; Wancourt Ridge; Second Scarpe; Second Passchendaele.
12 February 1918: Transferred as a Pioneer Battalion to the 66th Division.
During 1918: St Quentin; the Somme Crossings; Rosieres.
7 May 1918: Absorbed the personnel of 11th Battalion and transferred to 97th Brigade of the 32nd Division
31 July 1918: Absorbed the cadre of the 11th Battalion and continued to engage in various actions on the Western Front including: Cambrai; the Selle;
11 November 1918: Ended the war in France, near Avesnes.

2/4th (Cumberland & Westmorland) Battalion Territorial Force
October 1914: Formed at Kendal and then moved to Blackpool.
4 March 1915: Embarked for India from Avonmouth arriving at Bombay

31 March 1915 and remained for the duration of the war.

2/5th (Cumberland) Battalion Territorial Force

October 1914: Formed at Kendal.
November 1915: Moved to Falkirk and joined the 2/4th and 2/5th of the Royal Scots Fusiliers to form the 13th Battalion of the 194th Brigade of the 65th Division.
January 1916: Absorbed by the 2/4th Royal Scots Fusiliers.

3/4th and 3/5th Battalion Territorial Force

March 1915: Formed and then moved to Ramsey, Isle of Man.
8 April 1916: Became the 4th and 5th (Reserve) Battalion.
1 September 1916: The 4th absorbed the 5th as part of the East Lancs. Reserve Brigade.
January 1917: Moved to Ripon and then Scarborough, finally to Filey where it remained.

6th (Service) Battalion

August 1914: Formed at Carlisle as part of the First New Army and then moved to Grantham to join the 33rd Brigade of the 11th Division and then moved to Frensham.
1 July 1915: Mobilised for war and embarked for Gallipoli from Liverpool via Mudros.
20 July 1915: Landed at Cape Helles.
31 July 1915: Moved back to Mudros.
7 August 1915: Landed at Suvla Bay.
18 December 1915: Evacuated to Imbros due to heavy losses from combat, disease and severe weather.
1 February 1916: Moved to Alexandria to defend the Suez Canal.
30 June 1916: Embarked for France from Alexandria landing at Marseilles and engaged in various actions on the Western Front including: tWundt-Werk; Flers-Courcelette; Thiepval.
During 1917: the Ancre; Messines; Langemarck; Polygon Wood; Broodseinde; Poelcapelle.
9 February 1918: Disbanded in France at Mazingarbe.

7th (Service) Battalion

7 September 1914: Formed at Carlisle as part of the Second New Army and then moved to Wool to join the 51st Brigade of the 17th Division and then moved to Andover.

January 1915: Moved to Bovington and then Winchester.
15 July 1915: Mobilised for war and landed at Boulogne and engaged in various actions on the Western Front including;
During 1916: Albert; Delville Wood.
During 1917: First and Second Scarpe; Roeux; First and Second Passchendaele.
22 September 1917: Absorbed twenty-one officers & 239 men of the now dismounted Westmorland & Cumberland Yeomanry, and became the 7th (Westmorland & Cumberland Yeomanry) Battalion.
During 1918: St Quentin; Bapaume; Amiens; Albert; Havrincourt; Epehy; Cambrai; the Selle; the Sambre.
11 November 1918: Ended the war in Aulnove, France.

8th (Service) Battalion
September 1914: Formed at Carlisle as part of the Third New Army then moved to Codford to join the 75th Brigade of the 25th Division, then to Boscombe.
May 1915: Moved to Romsey and then Aldershot.
27 September 1915: Mobilised for war and landed at Boulogne and engaged in various actions on the Western Front including;
During 1916: Vimy Ridge; Albert; Bazentin; Pozieres; Ancre Heights.
During 1917: Messines; Pilkem.
During 1918: St Quentin; Bapaume; Estaires; Messines; Bailleul; First and Second Kemmel.
22 June 1918: Transferred to the Composite Brigade of the 50th Division.
7 July 1918: Disbanded in France.

9th (Service) Battalion (Pioneer)
September 1914: Formed at Carlisle as part of the Third New Army and then moved to Lewes and Seaford to join the 66th Brigade of the 22nd Division and then moved to Eastbourne.
February 1915: Became a Pioneer Battalion of the 22nd Division, then moved to Seaford, on to Aldershot.
4 September 1915: Mobilised for war and landed at Havre.
29 October 1915: Embarked for Salonika from Marseilles and engaged in various actions against the Bulgarian Army including;
During 1916: Horseshoe Hill; Machukovo.
During 1917 and 1918: Doiran.
30 September 1918: Ended the war in Macedonia, N.W. of Lake Doiran.

10th (Reserve) Battalion

October 1914: Formed as a service battalion at Southend as part of the Fourth New Army

10 April 1915: Became a 2nd Reserve Battalion and then moved to Billericay.

September 1915: Moved to Seaford as part of the 4th Reserve Brigade.

1 September 1916: Absorbed into the Training Reserve Battalion.

11th (Service) Battalion (Lonsdale)

17 September 1914: Formed at Carlisle by the Earl of Lonsdale and an Executive Committee, then moved to Kendal and Workington.

October 1914: Moved to Blackhall Racecourse, Carlisle and then on to Prees Heath to join the 97th Brigade of the 32nd Division.

June 1915: Moved to Wensley and then Fovant, Salisbury Plain.

27 August 1915: Taken over by the War Office.

23 November 1915: Mobilised for war and landed at Boulogne and engaged in various actions on the Western Front including;

During 1916: Albert; Bazentin; the Ancre.

During 1917: the Ancre and the pursuit of the German army to the Hindenburg Line.

During 1918: First Arras; Amiens; Albert; Bapaume.

10 May 1918: Reduced to training cadre with surplus personnel transferred to the 1/5th Battalion.

13 May 1918: Transferred to the 66th Division.

31 July 1918: Cadre absorbed by the 1/5th Battalion.

12th (Reserve) Battalion

Formed from the depot companies of the 11th Battalion at Prees Heath as a local reserve battalion in the 17th Reserve Brigade.

1 September 1916: Absorbed into the 75th Training Reserve Battalion.

Appendix 2

Further research and sources

The *Whitehaven News* (7 March 1918) gives a lot on background information about the overseas YMCA huts in general, and their furthest reaches at Jerusalem and Baghdad, not just near European battlefields. The University of Birmingham's Cadbury Research Library has a photograph of the location of YMCA huts near the French coast between Dunkirk and Le Havre. Sadly, there is not a key to the numbers which presumably indicate which hut was which.

Any visit to Kew Archives should be planned in advance. Go armed with evidence of who you are and where you live (if you don't have a driving licence, take a passport) but at the same time don't take too much – bags have to be stored in a locker. Possessions can be searched at any time and only graphite pencils (without erasers) may be used. Surprisingly camera phones can be used. Take pictures of the documents and look at them at home at ease: the archive room temperatures are freezing. Kew Archives was a combination of the faff and hassle at an airport and a supermarket frozen food aisle. Fleece next time…

Select Bibliography

Abel Heywood & Son's Guide Books Keswick and Derwentwater (Past Presented, 2006 – original edition c 1924)

Benjamin, Frederick *A Derwent Club Centenery 1879-1978*, (Derwent Club, 1978)

Cadbury Research Library, University of Birmingham

Caldbeck Characters (Caldbeck & District Local History Society, 1995)

Collingwood, W G *Elizabethan Keswick*, (Michael Moon, 1987; first published in 1912)

Cumbria Archive Service

Fell and Rock Climbing Club Journals, 1914, 1915, 1916, 1917, 1918, 1919

Gedding, Evelyn, *A Second Dip into Caldbeck's Past* (DKM Caldbeck, 1988)

Greenup, Richard, *A Walk Through Our Village of Caldbeck*, 2011 (Caldbeck & District Local History Society)

Keswick & Northern Lakeland (Dalesman, 1968)

Keswick Historical Society and the Friends of Keswick Museum and Art Gallery *Keswick Characters, volume one*, Keswick Historical Society and the Friends of Keswick Museum and Art Gallery (Bookcase, Carlisle, 2006)

Keswick Reminder, 30 June 1915 onwards

McNamara, Roy *Being Prepared, 100 Years of Scouting in Cumbria,* (Bookcase, 2007)

Nicholson, Norman *Portrait of the Lakes*, (1963 and 1972)

Pollock, John Charles and Randell, Ian, *The Keswick Story: The Authorized History of the Keswick Convention*, (undated)

Postlethwaite's Mines and Mining in the Lake District, John Postlethwaite (Michael Moon, re-print 1975)

Richardson, Keith, *The Greta*, Keith Richardson ((2012)

Robinson, Peter, *Railwaymen Remembered*, Cumbrian Railways Association (2008)

Shaw, W T *Mining in the Lake Counties*, (Dalesman, 1970)

Shepherd, Margaret E, *Across the Oceans – Emigration from Cumberland and Westmorland before 1914*, (Bookcase, 2011)

Sutton, Shelagh, *The Story of Borrowdale*, (Lakeland Productions, 1974 – first produced in 1961)

The Parish of Lamplugh (Lamplugh Parish Council, 1993)

The Story of St Kentigern's Crosthwaite Keswick by the Vicar (The British Publishing Company Ltd)

The War Work of Auxiliary Hospitals and Voluntary Aid Detachments of Cumberland, Westmorland, and part of North-West Lancashire, August 1914-1919 by H. G. G. (Titus Wilson, Kendal, 1921)

Trevelyan, John *The Cumbria Way*, (Dalesman, 1981)

Wainwright, Martin, *Wainwright: The Man Who Loved the Lakes*

War Work of Auxiliary Hospitals and Voluntary Aid Detachments in Cumberland, Westmorland and parts of North Lancashire

White, Bonnie, *Women's Land Army in First World War Britain*, St Francis Xavier University, Canada (1977)

Wrigley, C J *AJP Taylor: Radical Historian of Europe,* 2006

Yuan, Margaret Speaker, *Beatrix Potter,* (Kyle Zimmer, 2005)

Online sources

Wikipedia
Border-regiment-forum.com
Cumbria-industries.org.uk
Ancestry.co.uk
spartacus-educational.com
Stbees.org.uk
Livesofthefirstworldwar.org
The British Newspaper Archive
Keswickrailway.com
Patterdaletoday.co.uk
Ullswatermemorial.co.uk

Museums

British Library, London
Keswick Museum and Art Gallery
Millom Discovery Centre
Museum of Lakeland Life, Kendal
Cumbria's Museum of Military Life, Carlisle
IWM, London
The National Archives , Kew, London
Threlkeld Quarry & Mining Museum

Index